Be Courageous!

Liana Lim

MONDAY
NEVER COMES

LIANA S. SIMS

Freedom 2 Live

Editors: Chandra Sparks Splond and Michelle Anthony
Cover Design: Daven Baptiste for rcmtv.com

God is within her,

She will not fall;

God will help her at break of day.

(Psalms 46:5, New International Version)

CONTENTS

Introduction

On March 29, 2013, my life changed forever. It was Good Friday, the beginning of Easter weekend, and I was off from work. While sitting at my dining room table eating a bowl of Cheerios, I received a call and picked up the phone to hear my mother say, "Li Li, I tried to resuscitate your dad."

Immediately I began to hyperventilate. I fell to the ground, and all I had the strength to do was plead to my mom over and over, "What do you mean? What do you mean? What do you mean?"

I was no fool; I knew the meaning of *tried*. Tried meant unsuccessful. My mother had attempted to bring my dead father back to life, and her attempt failed. That one phone call changed everything for me. For thirty seconds, the world stopped spinning, everything stood still, and the greatest pain I had ever experienced had overtaken my heart.

My daddy died.

It was just that simple, that quick. My mom thought my dad overslept for work, only to find her husband in their bed, dead. Both she and my little brother tried to resuscitate him to no avail.

The story of my daddy's life ended on March 29, 2013. Sure, his life gets to live on through me and my three siblings and everyone who was blessed to come in contact with him, but his physical story here on earth ended that day. His journey had come to completion. For a reason unknown to me, it was determined that whatever work he was sent to this world to accomplish was completed.

The Power of Story

I think about my dad and the impact he has made on my life a lot. I think about how he was from the South and how his journey as a Black man in America was far from easy. I consider the hardships my immediate family has endured and how through the test of time, he never turned his back on us. With grace, he endured. He rode the waves of life and refused to allow them to take him out. He was a warrior—a silent warrior, but nevertheless, a true warrior.

Today I have one regret. I wish I had made my dad tell me his entire life's journey and that I had written it all down. Don't get me wrong, my dad was quite the storyteller, and those stories will live on through me and will be passed on to my children, but I wish I had been more intentional. I wish I had cherished every single moment as the rare commodity each was. I wish I had captured his story and held on to every single moment for dear life because that indeed is what each moment was—dear life.

Stories are powerful. Every day we are given the breath to live is ultimately another word, line, page, chapter in the book of our lives. Within them is the ability to heal, transform, redeem, validate, liberate, empower, encourage, celebrate, and educate. And the cool part about the story of a life is that there are no duplicates.

Your story and mine matter simply because they hold the greatest value ever—individuality.

The most valuable things in this world are those that are rare and hard to find. Conversely, the more common and easily accessible a stone, antique, or car is, the less each is worth. Consider the same for life—your life, my life, our lives. Each is valuable simply because there is no other story like yours. Your path is an original, and there will never be a copy of it. Your life has a purpose that only you can fulfill, and you've overcome obstacles that were unique to your path.

When the noise of the day is gone, and it's time to lay your head on your pillow, the silent truth remains: This is your journey, and no one ever can or will be able to live it for you. Your life is indeed priced far above rubies. It is one of a kind.

Though rare and never to be repeated, what I love most about the story of our lives is it transcends the individual and has the power to connect and meet others in the spaces of their lives. And while, we are unique, we have more in common in our journeys than we realize. I discovered this first hand when I started going to therapy.

A Time to Heal

After losing my dad, a range of emotions led me to my therapist's office. During therapy, one thing I have learned is I am not as alone, different, and crazy as I thought I was when I first stepped into her office. Some days I literally felt like, "This woman is a prophet. How does she know or understand me so well?"

Well, it turns out she was not a prophet. Rather, she had

experienced so much of life with so many people and had journeyed in her own life that the truth that was revealed in our time together was simply that we have more in common than we realize. In the individuality and uniqueness of our stories, there are also several common denominators that bring us all together.

Ultimately, I believe the two prevalent common denominators in each person's life are pain and love. So in this book, I choose to share fragments of the narrative of my life that reveal these two things. I am evolving. Therefore, this book or any book I ever write will not be able to contain my entire narrative, but I fight to give all that I have in this portion because of one fundamental belief I hold near and dear to my heart, which led me to write this book: *I believe in the power of story.*

Stories touch people, and I believe there is healing in the touch. When our stories are shared, they connect us to one another, and they give us the hope to keep living, to keep going, to keep fighting. It doesn't matter how we fight, but as Nike declares, "Just do it!" If it's through dance, music, film, photography, poetry, or some other art form, just be sure to share your story. Your individual, unique, rare and extremely valuable story matters.

My Story

At the age of twenty years old, I was five-five and weighed more than 350 pounds. I had been overweight since elementary school and progressed to battling obesity. This book is very near and dear to my heart because after naturally losing 180 pounds over the course of four years, I realized something about my story: It wasn't just *my* story. I realized it was a tool that was powerful enough to reach another human being—a regular everyday person.

Now, I am not exceptional. Most people say I am because of what and how I have overcome, but that's what I want others to understand. I am not special in that way. My life highlights the very opposite idea. I am a regular girl, and that's what makes me special. I share this in hopes I will inspire someone else to believe, to dream, to heal, and ultimately to thrive. I am the common man's inspiration because I, too, am the common man. I am only heroic to the degree that I stand out among the masses with a powerful, transformational story, but what's more powerful is that what I attained is not unattainable. I am a regular girl who decided to fight for her life. And you can too!

One day, I was on a retreat with some girls from college, and while at the top of a mountain I realized Monday was never going to come. "Monday" represents the perfect day or moment to take control of our lives and make change. I realized then there was never going to be that perfect day—that perfect moment—when I was all of a sudden ready to tackle life. That wasn't my reality, and I doubt it's yours either. And for many of us, we have denied ourselves the opportunity to live the life we really want because we're still waiting for that magical moment to appear.

So, what if that magical moment never appears for you? How long do you want to put off living, waiting for the perfect, comfortable moment in life to come and give you all the confidence you think you need in order to thrive? Well, here I am writing this book, and I can honestly say to you that moment never came for me, but I decided to take charge of my circumstances anyway. That being said, I share with you, pieces of me.

CHAPTER 1

THE MONDAY MENTALITY

I couldn't believe they actually called me.

On Monday, February 13, 2012, NBC's *The Today Show* offered me the opportunity to highlight my weight loss on their show. Just two days later, I was in New York. I could not believe the first time I was in New York was to be on national television, sharing my story about how I conquered obesity.

At one point in my life, losing five pounds was unfathomable for me, and in four years, I lost 180 pounds. Every time I think of how far I have come, I am amazed all over again. When I see the comparison pictures, I still can't believe this has been my journey.

I recall how weak and defeated I felt. I remember the

days I would literally cry and just hit my stomach feeling like it was the bane of my existence. I remember how trapped and overwhelming obesity was for me.

But there I was, sitting in my car listening to a voicemail from NBC offering me the chance to come to New York and tell the world about my journey to freedom. I couldn't believe this was actually my life, that I was being acknowledged for doing something remarkable in the world of weight loss.

The girl who spent most of her childhood being teased for being fat was now being acknowledged for conquering obesity. It's amazing how what seems like defeat at the end of the road can actually just be the first chapter to a beautifully written masterpiece—a story yet to be told.

So, off to New York I went. *The Today Show* hooked me up to say the least—paid for my plane ticket, sent a driver to pick me up from the airport, and booked my hotel just blocks away from The Rockefeller Plaza where I would be filming. I felt like I was living the life, like at any moment, I was going to wake up from this wonderful dream. Time and time again I kept thinking, *I can't believe this is really my life.*

When It Hit

I arrived in New York City on Wednesday afternoon, and that

night I met up with Aaron, my childhood friend from church, for dinner. The moment was simply wonderful, just eating good food and holding good conversation with a good person. Sometimes in the age of the Internet we can downplay the wonders of what occurs when two human beings just sit down, connect, talk, and engage in the moment with each other.

As we were enjoying our meal, my friend said, "Queen (my nickname), my girlfriend got me some running shoes." It was kind of cool. People often feel comfortable sharing their goals and aspirations with me, especially when it is fitness related.

I looked at him and I said, "Aaron, when are you going to start running?"

He paused and replied, "I would hate to say Monday."

"Because Monday never comes," I replied.

I had been working on this book to share pieces of my journey, but I had yet to determine what I would title it. It was in that moment that I knew I was going to title this book *Monday Never Comes*. I had been wrestling in my mind with what to call the book, how to approach it, what I would include, and what was unnecessary. There has been so much to my journey, and I knew I could not tell it all, yet I knew there was a story to be told.

Right there at dinner with Aaron, a confidence came over me. I knew with certainty that *Monday Never Comes* was the beginning of a movement. This was more than simply a book project. It is the way I hope to inspire people to live, to stop postponing their goals and dreams.

The Monday Mentality

How many times have you said one of these statements to yourself?

- I'm going to start on Monday.
- When the weekend is over, I'm going to get back on it come Monday.
- Monday I'll start over.
- Monday I'll get serious and focused.
- Monday I'm going to the gym and getting back on my diet plan. I'm going to eat all this bad stuff now because Monday, I'm going hard.

And how many times have you looked up and realized that Monday has come and gone and you didn't do what you said you were going to do?

Monday does not necessarily refer to the literal day of Monday. It's a metaphor for how many of us often approach life. I use Monday as the example because in the world of weight loss, you often hear about what is going to happen on "Monday," which is symbolic of any moment beyond right now. I call it the Monday mentality. Take it from someone who knows the Monday mentality all too well. We deceive ourselves. We convince ourselves that when Monday arrives, we will be ready, and there will be no turning back.

Monday is the false belief that perhaps at some other point in time, other than right now, you will have more motivation and more drive to complete the task ahead of you or to pursue the dream, vision, or goal you have for yourself. We delay our dreams and romanticize the future as if it offers us a unique ability to perform better than we would if we decided to live our dream today. However, you already have what you need to be an active participant in your goals, today. Don't put off until Monday—or any other day—what desperately needs to be done in the right now.

People often want to know what made me start this journey. I had been overweight for a very long time. I always wanted to lose weight but I never felt capable or strong enough. But eventually, I became desperate. I was afraid if something didn't change, I would live the rest of my life miserable. I had realized after more than ten years of struggling with obesity, the weight loss process had yet to become easy to engage. I came to the realization that Monday wasn't coming. I was determined to stop putting my life off, stop waiting until things got easy or convenient. If it never became easy, I had to make some changes. I had to engage the process and be willing to put up a fight for the sake of my own life, my dreams, my aspirations, my hopes, and my sanity.

I had to become an active participant in my own healing and journey to freedom from the bondage of obesity and the fear that I could never conquer. This is coming from the girl who didn't think she could lose five pounds. It was a process and not a quick fix, but along the journey I've learned a lot about myself, life, and what it takes to be victorious in the midst of great difficulty. Later on in the book, I further discuss my moment of change and how it set the trajectory for my weight loss journey.

No matter how unattainable your thing seems to you, it's only "seemingly impossible." However, you will never know it's really possible until you stop putting your life off. Those who conquer, succeed, win, and prosper are those who determine to throw away the Monday mentality and fight for their life now.

Welcome to my journey. Meet the girl who after fighting obesity for fourteen years had a God encounter at the age of twenty and has forever been changed. Join me as I share what took place the day I decided to change and some tools I have picked up along the way and allow the truth to penetrate your heart. It is my hope that when you are finished reading this book, you will hope again, trust again, believe again, fight again, and determine you are worth it just one more time.

After leaving New York and returning home from appearing on *The Today Show*, my experience caused me to realize everyone has the potential to overcome their fears and to pursue their dreams. I knew how "regular" I felt on the inside. I became overwhelmingly convinced I had a message to share because I knew many people would be able to relate to my story that there was something they needed to do and they probably felt like the odds were not in their favor. Like me, they probably counted themselves out time after time, and that's why I knew I had to speak up and spread my message.

Once the show aired, so many people were calling, texting, and leaving posts on my Facebook wall about how inspired they were. One lady would literally send me pictures of her going to the gym and making better food choices. Many people in my life began to pursue various goals that once seemed unattainable such as returning to school or starting a business. They expressed how knowing me and seeing my journey caused them to believe they too could be successful. I learned that overcoming my trials was not just for me, but it was to be shared so others could grow in their confidence as well. With a renewed passion and a sense of urgency, I returned home and continued writing this book.

My heart's deepest desire is that you will never put your life on hold, that you will face fear, abandon the Monday mentality, and go for it right now because Monday never comes.

CHAPTER 2

THE POWER OF YOUR WHY

I didn't know where I was going, but I knew I had to leave where I was. I struggled with my addiction to food and being overweight from elementary school until the age of twenty when I decided to seriously fight for my life. I had never met anyone who lost more than 100 pounds naturally. I knew people who had undergone weight-loss surgery, but there was no one I knew who took the day-by-day process of denying their flesh, sacrificing their immediate desires, and choosing the road less traveled. And honestly, that frightened me. It made conquering obesity seem impossible.

I didn't have a road map for losing at least 100 pounds

the natural way. I didn't have an example, no prototype or what my mentor would call a tire to kick. I had no one. Nobody could tell me how to fight this thing from experience. There were several people around me, especially at church, who struggled with obesity, but there were no mentors, no examples, and no giants who went before me to pave the way. I was lost, alone, scared, desperate, and seemingly hopeless. I wanted to get to a destination without even a compass to guide me, not a GPS or even a Thomas Guide atlas. What was I supposed to do?

There were a lot of health experts out there, but they were all skinny fitness gurus. They didn't understand me, my journey, or what I was about to face for the next four years of my life. They knew fitness, but they didn't know my addiction, the bondage I lived in daily, or the overwhelming fear that penetrated my heart and convinced me I would never, ever escape.

Concerned adults, doctors, and the health and fitness experts threw the facts at me all the time, but what many people never realized is that facts alone will not get a person to change or set them free from their bondage. Trust me, I knew the facts. I was well informed. Heck, I think I knew my condition better than anyone else. I lived it out every waking moment of my life. I was obese, I needed to get healthier, change my eating habits, exercise more, eat less, drink more water, etc. I was very aware of my state, so aware that it terrified me. Often, I simply suppressed the terror. What sense did it make to ponder on a reality I was convinced I didn't have the tools to change?

They made it sound so simple—just incorporate a new set of behaviors, and I would be set to go. If it were that easy, do you seriously think I would have been obese for so long? I needed more than a behavioral change. I needed a transformed, renewed mindset. I needed a complete paradigm shift, a brand-new set of eyes on how to see myself and the world around me. I needed tools that extended well beyond the world of medicine and scientific facts. I needed a reason to live and to fight for my life. I needed to know my why.

Take Me Back

It's funny that today I am a youth pastor because honestly I hated kids growing up. They made my life miserable and made me feel very small on the inside. I spent the majority of my childhood dodging bullets, navigating my day with the goal of prioritizing my sense of emotional safety. I didn't know at that time this was what I was doing, but as I look back over the years, I can see how my primary goal in life was to feel safe and not to be ridiculed and shamed by the people around.

However, something changed. When I was in high school, God blessed me with a best friend, Ashley Datcher. I met her at church. We became pretty much inseparable, and she provided a context of safety for me because she never judged me or made me feel inferior just because I was overweight. The relationship was very near and dear to me, and it helped me survive. I often felt insecure around other people but never around her. People at church nicknamed us Frick and Frack.

As I look back over those years, I realize even back then God was paving a way for me. I mean He truly sent my friend as an extension of His love for me. She helped me to survive what I considered to be hell, simply by her presence in my life. From the age of thirteen until my junior year in college, she was my rock. I never imagined a day would come where that friendship would shift. I couldn't comprehend a season where we would no longer be best friends, but God was up to something.

He wanted to do something radical in my life that would cause me to let go of any and everything that resembled comfort or a mechanism that allowed me to rely on anything other than Him. He was beginning to strip me of my crutches, and I was unaware of what was happening. While in college, Ashley and I started to grow apart. The transition of that friendship was very painful for me, and I didn't quite understand why I was losing my best friend.

What God had provided in the past to help me survive was no longer adequate for my new season where I was supposed to thrive, but it came at a great cost: my comfort.

Because of how kids treated me in relationship to my weight, over time I started to develop an unhealthy need for people to validate me and make me feel secure. Yes, we all need validation. In and of itself, that desire is not unhealthy. I believe we are created to be in relationship. However, my brokenness created an unhealthy need for security and safety and ultimately comfort. I was a kid full of life, but at the same time very afraid to actually live it.

In 2007, the same year I decided to face the greatest demon in my life (my obesity), my relationship with my best friend was altered. On the surface, it felt like I had lost my best friend to a guy. The relationship had changed her, in my opinion for the worse, and the more it was brought up, the further we grew. Everyone around us felt the same way I did about Ashley and her relationship, but I was most impacted because she was my best friend. I never thought our relationship would change.

Today we are better. Our relationship hasn't been restored to how it was in our childhood, but I think we have both resolved that no matter what, we will always be family and in each other's life. I have learned how to love people for who they are and not necessarily for who I want them to be. This perspective helps me to set my expectations for people appropriately and keeps me from experiencing extreme disappointment.

In the moment I had no idea the two were related, my weight loss journey and the loss of my best friend. I was angry and hurt with how our friendship had changed, but in hindsight, I now see the connection. I was so wrapped up in my pain and feelings of betrayal I didn't notice perhaps it was all part of God's greater plan and purpose for my life. I learned all things that seem bad are not necessarily bad but can be orchestrated or at least allowed by God to produce a greater good.

It doesn't mean it hurts any less in the moment, but it does help shape our perspectives on moving forward. Along this journey, I have faced many disappointments, but when I step back and look at the overall picture of my life, I can see how each one has served me well and has set me up for even greater opportunities in life. I had to press through those disappointments and not sulk in them for too long that I would miss out on what I was being prepared for in the next season. It has taken time for me to learn this lesson, and to be honest, I'm still learning it daily, but as I reflect on the loss of a best friend, I also see how it drew me closer to God and positioned me in a very vulnerable state that allowed me to open myself up to change. I lost something, but I gained as well. This is part of the circle of life.

When My Life Changed Forever

It was the spring 2007, and while I was wrestling with the pain of a broken friendship, I was, at the same time, considering perhaps there was something unique God was trying to do in my life and in my heart. Ironically, I was invited to go on a retreat with some girls who lived on my floor in the dorm. Naturally, I was opposed to the idea.

Let's just say, I was very culturally different from the girls who lived on my floor and was not typically down for engaging in activities with the majority of them. I was an urban black girl from Los Angeles attending an evangelical, conservative, white Christian school in the suburbs. Our worlds often didn't mesh. Though I was opposed to going, I was willing to take a risk because for a change, I was raw and open, honestly desperate for an encounter with God however it would come. I was very broken and vulnerable in this season and was willing to step outside of my comfort zone to encounter God. I went on the retreat, and I have never been the same.

While on the retreat, we participated in a meditation exercise. I'm going to be honest: As soon as they said we were going to meditate, I thought, *See, this is why I don't get down with the things these girls do,* but I was already in the mountains with them, and I had already made a promise to God that I was willing to be open and just engage in the process.

The meditation time required us to do an exercise on fear. We were instructed to go off alone and spend some time in prayer and to simply jot down our fears. I was at such a desperate place in my life; I didn't have a reason to hold back. It was just me and God, and for the first time, I wrote down my fears—all of them, even the ones I was ashamed to admit like my fear of people.

Every time my fear of people would arise in my mind in the past I would brush it off and think, *I am Liana.* This was my defense mechanism to try and convince myself that Liana isn't weak and to fear people is for the weak. Liana is not that girl. She is strong. So, with a bit of arrogance and false pride, I would cover my shame with the thought, *I am Liana.* My own pride and shame would not allow me to face the truth that people terrified me. That had been the case since elementary school.

The pain didn't subside, and I didn't grow out of it because I got older. If anything, it got worse, grew deeper, and my fear of people often controlled much of my social interactions. My goal in life became safety and survival. My daily life was focused on navigating my way throughout the day to surviving the darts that life threw my way. I simply wanted to make it home where I felt safe or in front of food where I was most happy and satisfied.

While on this retreat, I decided to put it all out there, to write down every single one of my fears that I could think of. My list included:

- Being lonely
- Traveling because of previous bad experiences of not fitting the seat belt on the plane
- Going to amusement parks because I didn't want to be ashamed if I didn't fit the ride
- People because I had been very wounded by my experiences with them
- Not knowing love, getting married, and having kids
- Being fat forever

- Not being good enough

- Losing sight of who I was. Not fully knowing how to differentiate between who was really Liana and who was the façade that helped me make it through the day

- Dying young

- Never feeling safe or fully accepted

- My future not being fulfilling but rather a continual grind

The list went on and on and on. At the end of the meditation time, I looked at my list, and for the first time, I noticed the majority of the fears were connected to one central factor: my obesity. It was the first time in my life I actually decided to completely and honestly face myself. I was very fragile and broken, but in that same moment, this sense of hope came over me in a way I had never experienced.

It's hard to explain, but it was as if God's presence was there to assure me this exercise was not done in vain. The image that comes to mind is as if I was laying on a table completely open in a hospital operating room. It was as if God was about to do an invasive surgery on me and my most vulnerable organs were exposed, but I didn't know He was about to do the surgery. I just knew I felt stripped naked, ashamed, and exposed, and this gentle comforting spirit rushed in to assure me the exposure was necessary for God, the master surgeon, to come in and do the necessary work in order to heal me. And for the first time, I was willing to endure the surgery because I was unwilling to remain in my sickness.

My pastor often says in describing seasons of his past, "I was so down I could jump up and touch the bottom of down." In so many words, until you are in a desperate place like I was, you won't take the necessary steps to pursue your own healing and freedom. No one needed to convince me I needed to engage the process. I knew how broken and desperate I was. Like I said before, I didn't know where I was going, but I knew I had to leave where I was. I made a declaration when I was leaving the retreat I would at least begin to make changes in the areas I knew needed change. I didn't have to know how I was going to lose all of the weight, but I could at least make the changes I was aware of.

Baby Steps

When I left the retreat, I began to make small changes. The first thing I did was take soda and juice out of my diet, and I began to drink water only. In the past I could easily drink two or three cups of soda while in the café for lunch or dinner. It was such a social hour that I could be in there with my friends for hours, just hanging and catching up on life. Before I knew it, I had taken in numerous calories worth of food and drink. So my first decision was to stop drinking my calories.

I made several gradual changes in my lifestyle, but it was less about eating better and more about a decision I had made to fight for my life and to be an active participant in my own healing. I will give you this nugget of advice: unless you're willing to be an active participant in your own healing, it will never occur. God will give you the tools to fight, but He won't pick them up and engage in the battle for you. He will be your strength in weakness, but you have to show up for the fight.

We All Need a Why

When I left the retreat and entered my daily life, I had a moment of realization. Now that I knew my fears and what was holding me back, I needed to have something that was greater than my fears that was going to help me to move forward in my journey.

People who know my weight-loss story often approach me and say, "Liana, I need you to motivate me." I look back at them and with all seriousness reply, "I can't motivate you. I can inspire you, but I can't motivate you. Motivation is internal."

This internal motivation, I like to call your why. If the why is powerful enough, you will succeed. The most important decision I made at the beginning of my weight-loss journey was to sit down and make a list of my whys. I suggest you do the same.

My Whys:

1. I want to be free! I feel shackled every day of my life both physically and emotionally, and I hate it.
2. I want to be confident and comfortable in my own skin.
3. I never want to get on an airplane again and not fit the seat belt.
4. I don't want to have to walk into an event and wonder if chairs are sturdy enough to hold my weight.
5. I hate walking into a room and mentally trying to figure out how I am going to navigate through the aisles and determine which ones I can and cannot fit down.
6. I want the freedom to be myself and not be ashamed of who I am.
7. I want to know that I put my best foot forward in life and came out as my best possible self.
8. I want to get married, have kids, and live a healthy and full life.
9. It's not just about the quantity of my years but the quality of them as well.

10. I want to feel comfortable with my body as I engage in a relationship with a man—to love and be loved deeply.

11. I don't want to hide anymore.

12. I don't want to be afraid anymore. I don't want fear to have the power to paralyze me.

13. I am more valuable than how I have treated myself.

14. I want to know that I can conquer anything.

15. I don't want to feel like an outcast.

16. I want to know and experience God's healing and freedom in every area of my life and live as a testimony to His power and glory.

17. I want to shop and wear the clothes I desire to wear, to be able to walk into a clothing store and not feel hindered by my size.

18. I never want to be on medications.

19. I want to be a Nike model.

20. I want to be the beautiful, courageous, ambitious girl that is hindered by the weight and shame of obesity.

Your why allows you to have a perspective like I did—you may not know where you're going, but you know you have to leave where you are. Your why has to have great depth and meaning to you. This isn't for anyone else. For a change, it's all about you.

Your why has to be strong enough to keep you on the journey, something you will read and re-read in times of discouragement or apathy (because both will come). It has to be deep enough that it will keep you going when you lack the desire to move forward, pick you back up when you have fallen off the wagon, and propel you to have hope for your future. It is ultimately the desired result that you want that makes all your sacrifices worth it.

Your why is your fuel, and no one can provide it for you. You have to have a personal resolve that makes this journey worth embarking upon. It doesn't require you to have an enormous amount of faith, just enough to put one foot in front of the other. As you continue to prioritize your why, choose to move out of a place of fear and complacency and become an active participant in your own growth, your faith will inevitably grow because you will begin to see yourself conquer in areas you once thought were impossible.

If you want to exit the Monday mentality, start with the basics. Lesson number one: Take the time to discover your personal why. It's your most powerful asset—your driving force.

This is not a process that is limited to weight loss. We all have our thing in life. In that season of obesity, my thing was surrounded by literal and emotional weight that I was carrying, but we all have that thing that feels impossible but we really want the courage to face. What is your thing? Once you are clear what that is, write down your list of fears. Next, write down your why—and make sure it's strong enough to counteract your fears.

All of the whys on my list ultimately sum up into one word: *freedom*. Today, as I write this book, I can honestly say I have been set free from obesity, shame, fear, inadequacies, low self-esteem, doubt, people's opinions of me, low standards, playing life safe, selling myself short, and hopelessness. I found my why, and I haven't let go since. If you don't read another word in my book, I hope you leave this chapter knowing you too have access to freedom. Determine your own personal why, and with everything in you, refuse to let go. As you continue to prioritize your why and move out of a place of fear and complacency and become an active participant in your own growth, your faith will inevitably grow because you will begin to see yourself conquer in areas you once thought were impossible.

My mentor once told me, "It's okay to be afraid. Put fear on your back like a backpack and just go. And as you see yourself conquering, the fear will decrease." Fear cannot be conquered in a vacuum. You can't get rid of fear and then face life. Only facing the fear will cause it to lose its power. But none of this will ever happen if you don't start with the basics. Lesson number one, take the time to discover your why.

CHAPTER 3

THE TRUTH ABOUT COURAGE

The first day I met my mentor, Dr. Nicole LaBeach, I remember thinking, *Who is this lady?* That day, back in 2005 she left an impression on me. She tends to say things in ways that I have never heard before, yet every time they make sense to me, and they become these life-altering moments. She often gives me advice in such a way that it shifts my entire perspective on how I view a thing, and subsequently, how I live. Well, this happened the very first day we met. I happened to be walking through the church with Brittany, one of the ladies from church who took me under their wing. While walking through the church, Brittany asked me to stop by Dr. LaBeach's office with her. At the time, I had no idea who Dr. LaBeach was, but today she could not get rid of me even if she wanted to.

While we were in her office, my mentor, who was a stranger to me at the time, began to inquire about my life and ask me all kinds of questions. It was quite interesting to me because she did not know me, yet she seemed genuinely interested. She said something to me that day that changed everything for me.

Put Fear On Like a Backpack

Before I met Dr. LaBeach, I thought fear was my enemy. I thought something was wrong with me because I was afraid all of the time and I allowed fear to hold me back. I didn't vocalize this to anyone because I was afraid to show my wounds, my issues, and my pain. I felt like walking around obese was vulnerable enough; it gave room for people to ridicule and make their judgments of me. It was how I had lived since I was a child.

Honestly, I was angry because I knew everyone had issues, but the difference was everyone could see my brokenness. I didn't like how I felt like I had a disadvantage in life. I didn't get to hide as much as other people, so I hid everything else. I didn't talk about my insecurities and my fears. I didn't talk about anything. I just did my best to survive, to dodge pain, and to keep myself around people who made me feel secure and wanted. I avoided taking risks, and I only went after the things in life that seemed possible. I was deathly afraid of failure. I already felt like a failure being obese, but I rarely acknowledged it because I felt hopeless and incapable of fixing it, so I just kept living the best I knew how.

One night in one woman's office changed me. The change wasn't immediate, but when I began my weight-loss journey, I remembered the conversation I had, and I took her up on her challenge to not let fear paralyze me but rather to put it on like a backpack and move forward. She asked me several questions about myself and what I wanted to do with my life. She could sense the fear and hesitancy in my response. I must admit I was wondering why she cared so much in the first place. Why was she so interested in my life? I still haven't figured that one out, but to this day, she hasn't stopped caring. Noticing the fear, reservation, and timidity I carried, she said to me, "It's okay to be afraid. Put fear on your back like a backpack and just go. And as you see yourself conquering, the fear will decrease."

At first I didn't understand. This woman just told me to put fear on like a backpack. She said, "Liana, just go. Live. Throw it on your back and just go. As long as you don't allow the fear to stop you, you'll be fine. As you go, it will decrease." A few years later, when I decided to start losing weight, I could hear her voice in my head saying, "Just go. Put the backpack on and go. It's okay to be afraid."

Up until that point, no one had ever told me it was okay to be afraid. I believed my job was to get rid of fear—to fight it. I always seemed to believe fear was stronger than I was. I backed down. I hid. I didn't show my fears, but I was very afraid. Over the course of time, I have come to realize her point. The only thing that fights fear is movement, momentum, living in the face of it. Fear cannot be conquered in a vacuum. You can't get rid of fear and then face life. Fear loses its power when movement and activity are present in the midst of life. When I began my weight-loss journey, I was very afraid. However, the difference was I decided to try, to take a step, and as I went, I began to lose the weight.

The more weight I lost, the less afraid I became. If you don't move, fear has won. So I've decided I will always put fear on my back like a backpack and just go.

Fear and Courage Are Not Enemies

One of my favorite Bible stories is about a man named Joshua. His story encourages me because I feel a lot like him. Joshua had a mentor named Moses who was the leader. God had given Moses the task of leading an entire nation out of slavery and into a promised land that God had chosen for them to inhabit. However, on the journey, Moses died, and Joshua was left to complete the task God had commissioned Moses to do. It was not Joshua's responsibility to lead the nation into the land. And if I were Joshua, this new mission would have scared me. But God knows us so well that He prepares us for what's ahead.

The first set of instructions that God gives Joshua is to be strong and courageous. He tells Joshua it is now Joshua's responsibility to get the people into the Promised Land and God's desire is that Joshua be courageous. Joshua was blindsided. He had no idea his leader would die, but since it happened, it became his responsibility to assume the role of leader. Of course God's instructions to Joshua are to be courageous because he had every reason not to be. His natural inclination was fear, and knowing He would respond in fear, God encourages Joshua, "Be courageous!" Out of all the things God could have said to Joshua, He simply said, "Be strong and courageous."

Like Joshua, there's a task ahead of you that you need to fulfill, and fear cannot get the final say. However, the presence of fear alone is not an issue. The issue is what you do with the fear or rather what you allow the fear to do to you.

I believe courage is not the absence of fear, but rather the decision to do it afraid.

The issue is not fear. It's when you allow fear to paralyze you and keep you from doing what must be done. Just have a little more faith than fear. Have enough faith to take the step that fear is begging you not to take. Courage is when you look fear in the face and say, "Today, we are going forward." Courage is putting on the backpack.

Joshua had an entire nation of people looking to him for direction. He could not afford to allow his fear to get the final say. He had to rise up in the face of fear and choose to be courageous, choose to not allow his insecurities or his hesitancies to keep him from going the distance. If we are honest with ourselves, you and I are just like Joshua. We are not those people who never get afraid and are always bold. No, like Joshua we get deathly afraid, we wonder if we have it in us to do the task in front of us with success. We back away a little because what it takes to accomplish what we must honestly scares us.

However, Joshua had to determine what was at stake was not worth him backing down for. You and I must make that same decision every single day of our lives. We must ask what we will lose if we allow fear to win and consider the cost of being a coward. Is it worth it? There was an entire nation depending on Joshua, and he needed to make a decision. I argue the decision he needed to make wasn't to not fear. It was to determine courage was his only route. Courage is facing your fear, not backing down to it. It's putting on the backpack and moving forward, trusting that fear will not take you out. There is always something at stake. It may not be a nation but I guarantee there is always a cost to giving up.

Others Are Watching

I remember when my daddy died in 2013. I honestly didn't know some days if I could make it—if the pain was so unbearable it would take me out. There were days I was afraid to live. I went to sleep crying—I cried all night long and would wake up crying. I was afraid to keep going.

Then I remembered I was a youth pastor. I had many young people who were watching how I lived my life. They were watching to see what faith looked like, what it looks like for life to hit hard, and whether I was going to allow it to destroy me.

I would consider my students and I would get out of the bed, take a shower and face the day. I had to—like Joshua—determine the cost was just way too high. I didn't get to just not fight. There were lives that were attached to mine, and they were so valuable to me I decided to put the backpack on just one more time.

Before I lost my dad, I thought losing more than one hundred pounds was the hardest, scariest thing I would have to do. I have learned since then, it just isn't the case. Life will always be happening, and as long as it is, there will be fears to face, embrace, and overcome. Fear challenges me to go the extra mile. It's a sign I am still living; it provides an opportunity for internal growth. I don't believe we should live in a state of fear. I just believe we shouldn't be overwhelmed by its presence. We should embrace it as a part of life and ultimately as that part that doesn't get to paralyze us. It only gets to show us what we're really made of. Fear gives me the chance to be courageous.

I Embrace Fear

I used to only go after things I thought I could do. I didn't take risks because I was afraid of failing and feeling defeated. Therefore, I played life safe. My weight-loss journey became the beginning of change. It didn't happen overnight, but I now embrace fear a little bit better than I did in the past. It is a very uncomfortable experience. However, it's an indication for me that I am going after something big, something out of my reach, something that will stretch and grow me. I am learning it's about where I place my fears and what I choose to do with them.

Do I hand them over to a very capable God, or do I allow them to turn into anxiety?

Fear does two things to me: (1) I get extreme anxiety or (2) I allow it to be an opportunity to trust God with my life. The more I trust God, the more risk I take in life. Now, I dream big, and I have this attitude that says, "God, I will jump. And I am only jumping because I trust You will catch me." God is going to catch me or He is going to give me wings to fly, but one thing is for sure, my faith has grown to the point that I believe I will never hit the ground.

Even those moments that feel like I hit the ground—like when I didn't make the cut for *The Biggest Loser*—these are just times that feel that way. My feelings are temporary, but the truth is lasting, and here I am today, still going. I didn't make the *The Biggest Loser*, but God had another plan in store for me and that plan still includes me soaring. It was a plan that came with pain and disappointment, but it taught me how to trust Him even more, how to take risks, and how to keep jumping, trusting I will never hit the ground.

As a result, I am a different person today. I dream bigger. Honestly, there's no way I would ever think I would be a pastor. I am a twenty-eight-year-old female pastor. And what's crazier is I am a youth pastor. Kids made my life miserable, and here I am pastoring kids. It's like God used my experience as a youth pastor to help heal me and restore my childhood.

I never knew I would have a story to tell. I definitely didn't think I would have the discipline to write a book and publish it (and it won't be my last).

I learned as a teenager I loved to speak, but I was always so insecure about how I appeared to people. Now, that's when I feel most alive. I want to spend the remainder of my life traveling and using my voice to inspire and deposit hope into people.

Currently, I am preparing to apply to go back to school to get my doctorate in psychology. Me, Liana, get a doctorate? I am very afraid I don't have what it takes to go back to school and manage the life I have, but I have to because deep inside I want to, and though I am afraid, fear alone is not a good enough reason for me not to put on the backpack.

I want to offer people the type of healing my therapist has offered me, and it is worth me going after, fear and all. I counted the cost, and it is worth it. We must learn to embrace fear as part of the journey.

Fear is not our enemy. It is an opportunity for growth. It challenges us to rise to the occasion and to trust God with our lives. Fear is a sign to me I am living and not just existing.

The Faith Factor

Ultimately, I believe faith is the opposite of fear, and they both can't have dominion inside of you. I once heard it said, "You have two beasts living inside of you: fear and faith. The one that wins is the one that you feed the most." You beat fear with faith.

I mentioned before the presence of fear is not a bad thing. The only way to not allow fear to win is to have enough faith to defeat it. Well, faith is built in two ways. Most of this chapter I spoke about courage. Courage is when you decide to do it afraid. Thus, the more you see yourself going after the things that scare you, the greater your faith becomes because you realize the obstacle or the task before you wasn't really worth being afraid of in the first place. As a result, having courage helps to build your faith.

There is also this powerful tool we have called the human memory. What's the point of winning the previous battles if we don't remember we have once beat them? Remembering what we have overcome in the past helps us to fear less about what we face in the future.

Faith is built by remembering past victories. Over and over in the Bible, God instructs His people to remember—remember what He had done for them in the past, the victories they had gained, battles overcome, miracles witnessed, hardships that didn't destroy them. Why was God telling them to remember? Well, God knew there would be more difficulty ahead and that when faced with fear, they would need to remember what God had brought them through.

When relying on God's track record, it gives a confidence to face the unknown—the scary things of life. Courage plus memory equals faith. Courage causes us to rise in the face of fear, then we are to remember the previous obstacles to give us a confidence that says, "If it didn't take me out last time, it won't take me out this time." Faith helps us to overcome the power of fear.

CHAPTER 4

ONE DECISION AT A TIME

One day while conversing with a woman about my weight loss, she mentioned her desire to lose weight as well. I looked at her and said, "Do want to know how I lost my first fifty pounds?"

With excitement and anticipation she exclaimed, "Of course!"

She was waiting for me to give her the secret, as if there was a huge mystery I had the answer to so she could run off and lose those unwanted pounds.

I looked her in her face and said, "You lose fifty pounds five pounds at a time." I think my response disappointed her. The only way I was able to lose 180 pounds was pound by pound. There's no secret to discipline and consistency.

On this journey to a healthier, more joyful Liana, I have

learned not to despise humble beginnings. They often set the trajectory for the rest of the journey.

One of my favorite shows on television is the Shonda Rhimes' hit *Scandal*, starring Kerry Washington. Everyone loves Washington's performance right now, but I recall when she was in the movie *Save the Last Dance*. She performed well, and yet no one really noticed. I'm sure that leading up to this point in her now successful career, Washington took on several small, seemingly insignificant roles. However, taking those small roles and choosing to remain faithful on her path to being the actress she is today are what made the difference.

If she weren't diligent in what may have felt like small beginnings, she surely wouldn't be successful in the major roles in which she is currently excelling. Likewise, the decision to be diligent and faithful in small changes at the beginning of my journey paved the road to the woman I am today—180 pounds lighter and enjoying life.

Small Steps

As I mentioned earlier, my first decision of change was to stop drinking soda. If I wanted a particular drink other than water, it was something I really desired, and it was a treat. By the way, that drink was normally a soy chai latte. To this day, I still love soy chai lattes, iced or hot.

Next, I stopped eating fast food, unless it was Subway, Chipotle, El Pollo Loco or one of the other few healthy fast food options. I was living in an apartment across the street from campus, so I decided to start grocery shopping and cooking my own meals. Occasionally, I would eat in the cafeteria, but instead of burgers and fries, I went for the salad bar, chicken, veggies, and foods that were healthy and high in protein or fiber. I stayed clear of my favorite weaknesses such as root beer floats and French fries.

Another small change I made was buying a bike. Instead of driving to school, I began riding my bike. Small, gradual changes really added up and impacted my weight loss. When I began my journey, during the spring of 2007, I was wearing a size twenty-eight. By my twenty-first birthday, just six months later, I was in a size twenty-two. Before my own eyes, I was doing what I once thought was impossible.

Small beginnings lead to lifelong victories. It isn't necessarily about how big the task or goal is that you're approaching, but rather a decision to be dedicated and committed to whatever it takes to gain ownership of your life. As you see yourself conquering in one area, you will begin to believe in yourself and over time begin to take on larger tasks. Eventually, your performance level will begin to match the season you are in. Your abilities will increase with each step you take—each decision to move forward and to push past fear, doubt, fatigue, and discouragement.

Block out the negative voices in your head that tell you you can't do this because the truth is you can and you are. We conquer one decision at a time. I am learning to allow each season to take its full course. There's no rush. As long as you are moving in the right direction, you are on track. I've learned the power of taking life one step, one goal, one meal, one workout session, and one breath at a time.

The Anxiety of the Unknown

In December 2011, I was finishing up my last semester of graduate school. I had no clue what I was going to do post-graduation, and initially, that thought was a bit disturbing. It was pretty overwhelming. The assignments were flowing in, and for some reason, I started experiencing problems with my body and mind I had never had before. A friend of my mine who was studying to get her doctorate in psychology said it sounded like anxiety, and to top that off, I would wake up in the morning feeling extremely down for no reason.

I was battling anxiety and depression at the same time, and it was a pretty scary feeling. This was a new experience. It caused great degrees of fear in me. Here I was about to graduate, clueless of my next step, and I was having issues with my body I couldn't seem to control or make go away. I was in a tough spot, and I needed relief.

I recall a point of transition. I made a deliberate choice to not focus on what was next in life. I had a sense God was encouraging me to simply focus on graduation. I believed the next step would become clear when it was necessary. This was a new kind of faith for me. I am the type of girl who likes to have a plan. I like to map out where to go next and how I'm going to get there. Sure, I trusted God to help me make the plan. However, this time God was challenging me to trust Him in a whole new way. Much like my entry into the weight-loss journey, God was asking me to trust Him with the unknown and to focus on taking the necessary steps at that particular point. I needed to invest my energy in my present circumstance—completing my final semester of my master's program.

Before I knew it, shortly after graduating, the position for youth pastor opened up at my church. Now, three years later, I am telling you this story. And as I am writing this book, I am already creating goals for the next step in my life and wondering about how I am going to proceed. Every now and then I have to slow down and remind myself that today—right now—I am living yesterday's dream. Yesterday, I wondered if my church would hire me as a youth pastor and today I am living it out and loving these kids.

At one point I was stressed, worried, overwhelmed, anxious, and afraid. Before I knew it, the circumstances of my life had changed, and what was once a desire of my heart became the reality of my everyday life. The lesson learned in this experience crosses over to every area of life. It is critical to consider today in lieu of yesterday.

Honor the Journey

Living well today requires me to fully appreciate my yesterday. Slow down and honor the journey. Goals are good to have, but if I am in a perpetual goal-setting mode, I miss out on celebrating the accomplishments I've already made. Sometimes we have to slow down long enough to appreciate where we are today. If all my attention is focused on setting new goals for tomorrow, I miss out on the reality that today I am living in yesterday's dream.

When I weighed three hundred pounds, all I could think about was seeing a two on the scale. When I weighed two hundred pounds, all I could think about was seeing a one on the scale. Something was missing if my entire focus was on the next leg of the journey. There was more than one hundred pounds of victory I wasn't focused on because I wanted to weigh less than two hundred pounds. The destination is not all that matters. The greatest joys in this process are what I have learned about myself on the journey.

Yes, I enjoy setting a goal and seeing myself accomplish it, but what actually gives me the fuel to believe I can set a goal and do well is all the previous goals I've set along the way, the countless victories that got me from one leg of the race to the next.

I often ask women, "How much weight do you want to lose?" They become so overwhelmingly focused on and afraid of the distance between where they are and where they desire to be that they often miss the beauty of the baby steps required to actually reach their destiny.

What I want each person to realize is every mountain you climb in life requires one step, one climb at a time. You reach the top because of the accumulation of the steps you took in order to get there. The five pounds we often minimize in the weight-loss journey ought to be more prized than how they are often treated. Be careful not to just skip over those five pounds as if they are meaningless. Celebrate them. It's five pounds away from obesity and closer to your destination. It is five pounds farther away from yesterday and five pounds closer to a glorious tomorrow. Learning to rejoice in the battle is crucial to continual success. Appreciating the process is extremely valuable.

I mean no offense to anyone who has undergone surgery, but I often encourage people to take the natural route to weight loss. There is so much you learn about yourself when you are privileged to see yourself conquer what once seemed impossible and unrealistic. That sort of personal pride and sense of accomplishment only occurs when you are able to witness and revisit a process.

I often reread journal entries and scroll through pictures of my weight loss from over the years simply to remind myself of how I persevered through hardship, stayed the course when I wanted to quit, and overcame hurdles that felt like they were going to take me out. The process allowed me to grow in confidence. What I call my belief factor in myself has developed beyond what I could have ever imagined.

This process is so much more than about just losing weight, but I would not have known if it happened quickly or overnight. I learned this truth by overcoming one day, one decision at a time. Today you celebrate because yesterday you had a dream. I am who I am today because in 2007, I was a girl with a dream. My entire focus was centered around my desire to be set free from the impact that obesity had on me.

I Am the Hero

The year 2008 was epic for me. At twenty-one years old, I had lost one hundred pounds all by myself. I was a walking miracle. When asked, who my hero was, I quickly responded, "The 356-pound version of Liana." I have a relatively short list of heroes, and she most certainly belongs on it. Why am I my own hero? That may sound a bit egocentric, but it isn't. It's revolutionary. The woman I am today is a direct result of a decision I made back in 2007.

I can't celebrate the wonderful results I have achieved if I don't stop long enough to value the choice I made to enter the weight-loss adventure. I often encounter people who have lost weight, and when they look back on the heavier versions of themselves, they are disgusted. They are ashamed, embarrassed, and uncomfortable with the image of what they used to be. That's not my story. I give all the credit of who I am today to a very broken, wounded but courageous young lady who made a decision to fight for her own life.

I was afraid but I was desperate.

I didn't have a road map but I had a resolve.

My mom is so proud of my journey. One day she said to me, "Li Li you had a resolve and you changed your life."

I decided to live in vision versus in my circumstances. I took a chance on myself. When is the last time you took a chance on yourself? It can change the entire trajectory of your life. It's worth the risk. I hear my big brother Vick in my head saying, "No risk. No reward." That motto embodies the mentality I had entering the journey.

The years 2007 and 2008 were years of gradual change. I did not use a quick-fix diet. I learned to take small steps in the right direction. I made changes over time:

- I began to walk more, park farther distances, and use the stairs instead of the escalator or the elevator.
- I picked up a swimming class at school.
- I stopped eating heavy meals late at night. If I wanted a heavier meal such as a burger or pizza, I ate it around noon instead of 8:00 P.M.
- I would only eat fried food once a week. My favorite meal was fried fish and French fries.

- I didn't count calories. However, I became much more conscious of my caloric intake. For example, I started to look at the back of a package to see how many calories were in the item to determine if it was worth eating. I never knew one muffin could have six hundred calories until I started doing this. It caused me to become more conscientious of what I was putting in my mouth.

- I bought a gym membership and incorporated a buddy system in my life. Some days I would work out alone, but other days I would have friends go to the gym with me for a sense of accountability.

- I decreased my portions of breads, pastas, and rice, and I increased my portions of fruits and veggies.

- When I wanted sweets, I made deliberate decisions as to what I would have and I put limits on myself. In the past, I didn't limit myself. If I wanted it, I ate it. I learned to tell myself "no" and "enough" while still allowing myself to enjoy some treats. I have heard people say food is only designed to be nourishment for your body. However, I disagree. God would not have given us taste buds if we were not supposed to enjoy the taste of food as well. We have to learn to give ourselves limits.

Difficult Isn't Impossible

Everything happened gradually and over the course of time. I honestly believe this method is why I continued to lose and maintain the weight loss. It hasn't been a perfect journey, but it is one I have sustained. I had my seasons where I would gain a little and had to lose it again. That's a reality of the battle.

I struggle with food addiction, so I fall off the wagon but I never stay there. I remember my why, gather myself, and I hop back on the saddle because no matter how difficult the weight-loss process has been, nothing has been more difficult than living life obese. Perspective is everything.

One of my life's mottos has become, "Difficult isn't impossible." As humans, we are comfortable with excelling in areas that come naturally easy for us. If it's not a part of our natural set of gifts or talents, we often submit to the idea that perhaps it's not for us to do well. We are taught to pursue those things that are attached to our natural abilities and do well in. What happens when what you want doesn't come easy? What if it never becomes easy? Do you simply accept that it's impossible to excel? I hope not.

Losing weight has not been easy. Denying my desires to eat what I want, when I want, and in whatever quantity I desire is a daily struggle. However, I have decided not conquering in this area equates to a miserable life. I have concluded my goal is not to pursue those things that are easy. No, I have chosen to go after what is possible. I have readjusted my paradigm in thinking for my life and my pursuits. Difficult doesn't equate to impossible, and as long as it's possible, it's worth pursuing. I have come to realize all things are possible.

The Power of Choice

Since the battle is conquered one decision at a time, this means you have to start. You must realize the power of choice and the momentum that's gained solely off making that first decision to begin. So much or so little can happen in any given amount of time.

We often waste much time complaining about what we don't think we can accomplish. Time just passes us by, and we look up and realize nothing was done at all. It's like the forty-year-old woman afraid to go back to school, telling herself she is just too old to go to college. She was in school before, but life took a turn, and she never completed it. Now, she is in a place in her life where she can potentially go back to school, but she is just too afraid. Thoughts like, *I'm too old and not smart enough* race through her mind. The feeling it's too late and her time has passed at the chance for a college degree overwhelms her. The reality is her desire to obtain her degree is not going to cease and time isn't going to slow down. She is focusing on the one thing she can't control—time—and too little time focusing on what she can control—her decisions.

Time is going to keep ticking, and the only thing that will change is she will get older. She still won't have her degree, and she will still be unhappy about that reality. Many of us can relate. For one reason or another, we put off what we desperately want because we convince ourselves we don't have the resources necessary to succeed.

Often, time is the resource we don't think we have enough of. The truth of the matter is time isn't changing. What we do with it is the only thing we have control over. Sure, that woman may be forty, but if she doesn't get her degree now, she will look up and will be forty-five wishing she had her degree, and her excuse will be the same, "I am too old."

Don't put off until tomorrow what desperately needs to be done today. Don't lie to yourself and accept the idea that your time has passed. Your deepest desires are not going to subside just because you've convinced yourself difficult is impossible.

There were so many times I wanted to lose weight, but I allowed the fear that I couldn't do it and the enormous amount of weight I needed to lose to hold me back. When I decided to believe and to give myself a chance at winning, I lost one hundred pounds in one year, and in four years, I lost 180 pounds. That is huge to me because many years had passed without any significant change, and in one year, I did what I believed in the past was quite impossible.

Think about it. Time is going to continue to progress, but the difference is the choices we make with the time we are given. Our choices can be powerful and life changing, or they can be weak and produce deadness in our lives.

My pastor often says, "We all make a choice. Even the decision not to choose is a choice itself." There really isn't such a thing as indecisiveness. Our lives are a compilation of choices. Every moment moving forward is contingent on the previous decision we've made and the decisions yet to be made. We have more power in our own lives than we really think. Our perspectives and subsequent actions are all wrapped up in one tiny word, *choice.*

Disbelief is a choice.

Apathy is a choice.

Giving in to fear is a choice.

Complacency is a choice.

Accepting our conditions as permanent is a choice.

I run into people all the time who are so afraid of failure they simply don't choose themselves. I was that person. For many years, I didn't choose myself. And as a result, I made a choice. I chose to remain stuck, bound, and defeated. I was paralyzed by fear. However, the course of my life was forever changed by also making a choice to step out on faith, to win, to no longer surrender my life to fear and defeat, to be free from bondage, and to get up and do something about the circumstances of my life that were suffocating me. I decided to choose hope over defeat, faith over fear, courage over timidity, myself over the lie of who I thought I was.

Ever since childhood, I never believed I was special. I accepted the lie that I wasn't exceptional. I didn't know my value or worth. I often compared myself to other people and sought value in their opinions of me. I never had a real idea of what I wanted to do with my life. I often felt misplaced in the world, afraid to fail. Because of my past wounds and the fear of the unknown, I typically made very safe decisions. I avoided adventure, and I ran from uncertainty. But one day, I realized how unhappy

I was with the state my life was in, and I made a choice different than any other I had ever made. I made a choice to do something different. I encourage you to do the same.

A Step of Faith

Step out on faith and make a choice to move forward with your aspirations. You will never know if you can actually be successful unless you take the step of faith. Believe in yourself enough to take risks. Belief predicates sight. We will never see until we choose to do what is necessary for the future to unveil itself. Live as if you have confidence in your own future. See with your imagination so that in the natural you can make the choices necessary for your imagination to become reality.

I had the audacity to believe I could lose the weight while I was still 350-plus pounds. I didn't have an idea of what I would be like 180 pounds lighter, but I moved in that direction regardless. What I did know was I hated every aspect of being obese, and that was enough fuel to get me going.

And here I am now, sharing my story with you. Each and every one of our lives is a story yet to be told. What do you want your story to say? What do you want the world, your children, and future generations to know about your life? Ultimately, how do you want your story to read? What do you want God to say about the time He gave you on this earth?

Don't simply read this book, put it down, and say, "Oh wow, that was inspiring." I didn't write this book to simply inspire you. I wrote it to evoke change, to encourage you to no longer put your life off. I want to encourage you to make whatever choice necessary for you to live your best life. I used to be afraid to live—deathly afraid. I was afraid to be myself and to love myself. I used to think I was not strong enough to face the world. I believed I was weak and extremely incapable. For years I lived trapped. That is no longer my story, and I don't want it to be yours either. Take out the time to really consider your life.

Are you living or are you simply existing?

What desperately needs to be done today that you are putting off until another time?

Now is always your moment. Don't delay your goals until tomorrow, next month or the new year. Don't bank on a different moment in time being any different from today. Be willing to make the decisions that are pertinent to the life you want. It's your choice, but just remember *Monday Never Comes.*

CHAPTER 5

POWER OVER ADDICTION

My therapist said to me one day, "Liana, be compassionate toward your desires while you redirect your behaviors." Basically, don't beat up on yourself for having a struggle. Instead focus on the healthy decisions you can make toward overcoming. I realize I had an unhealthy relationship with my weaknesses. Instead of just embracing them, I would judge and be hard on myself for having the weakness in the first place.

But my therapist taught me that day it was possible to overcome in the face of great levels of difficulty without being so hard on myself about the reality of the struggle.

My Confession

I have an addiction.

I don't know where it came from, and I don't know if it will ever go away, but I have come to accept I am addicted to food. I used to be ashamed to think or voice this truth because I wasn't accustomed to people expressing or validating the reality that someone can actually be addicted to food.

I figured if I told people I believed I had an addiction they would see me as just making excuses for my lack of self-control. I used to be afraid to seek help or verbalize my struggle because I felt like I got myself into this hole, therefore it was my duty to get myself out of it. Over time I realized this is actually not true. It dawned on me one day if people don't believe I have an addiction to food then perhaps that simply means they don't struggle with food addiction. It's as simple as that. People often have trouble validating what they don't understand or what they've never experienced. I stopped looking for validation from people and decided to move forward with owning my story and learning how to excel in the midst of it.

When I was a kid, I used to watch talk shows like *Jenny Jones*, and they would have individuals come on and talk about their relationship to food. Some would say they ate when they were stressed, lonely, afraid, overwhelmed, sad, or depressed. Over and over, I would try to figure out if I related to any of their experiences. I connected to overeating, loving food, and the horrible experience of being obese, but I couldn't identify one area in my life that caused me to eat.

In 2007, when I decided to face myself and the reality of my obesity, I once again tried to figure out the cause—the source of when and why I ate excessively— yet, I couldn't seem to find one. It wasn't like there was a particular mood I was in when I ate. I simply love food. I eat when I am happy, sad, lonely, joyful, anxious, and at peace. I don't need a reason to eat. It's fulfilling and enjoyable, and that alone is my reason. I have a tug, sensation, continual desire that isn't connected to any other factor I can think of. I call myself an equal opportunity eater. It's just my thing. Everybody has their thing, and mine so happens to be food. I wish I could just shut if off. I wish it did not have the tug on me like it does. I wish I could shut off the cravings I have constantly. I wish it were easy.

Even though facing my addiction has been extremely difficult, I have had some help along the way. The type of help I encountered is so amazing because it's available for everyone. Yes, it's even available for you. God has been my greatest aid, and

He has given me the necessary tools to conquer my addiction. There were many times I asked God to remove my addiction—to make it easier. To date, He has yet to do so, but what He has given me is empowerment, which has enabled me to lose 180 pounds. He has given me His grace. God alone has consistently been my strength in the midst of utter weakness.

I Am Not Alone

I find great comfort in knowing some of the great spiritual pillars in the Bible faced some of my everyday struggles. The Apostle Paul had a "thing" too. He had something that seemed to be the bane of his existence. The Bible is not explicit in sharing Paul's particular struggle, but whatever it was, he described it in a way I can relate to.

Paul said, "Three times I pleaded with the Lord about this, that it should leave me. But he said to me, 'My grace is sufficient for you, for my power is made perfect in weakness.' Therefore I will boast all the more gladly of my weaknesses, so that the power of Christ may rest upon me" (2 Corinthians 12:8-9, English Standard Version).

Paul asked God several times to make it better, and God didn't make it better the way Paul wanted him to. Think of the area in your life where you are struggling. Place yourself into Paul's shoes. Imagine begging God to remove the pain, the distress, the trouble area you continuously present before Him to remove.

Wouldn't life be so much easier if God simply removed your thing? Well, God gave me and Paul the same answer. "No. No, I am not going to remove it, but I will give you everything you need to win in the face of it." He said, "I will give you grace, and I will be every ounce of strength you need."

Over and over we find this same theme displayed in the lives of people. God may not remove the trouble in your life, but He promises to equip you to face the battle. Our job is to show up, to be present, to be alert, and ready to use God's tactics and to remain utterly aware of the fact that everything you face in life, God is already two steps ahead of you, and He has equipped you with what is necessary to overcome. If we never chose to show up to the battle, how will we ever know that God has already positioned us to win?

In order for me to conquer my addiction to food, I have to be actively present in the affairs of my own life. There is no such thing as sitting on the sidelines and observing God work as if I am a spectator watching the game of my own life. On the contrary, I have to choose to engage, to position myself in a way to receive God's strength, insight, direction, motivation, empowerment, and technique. These are all tools crucial for me to be able to overcome daily.

Sufficient Grace to Overcome

God gives us grace in the face of our struggle and comes alongside with the promise that no matter what, He is ultimately our strength, if we so choose to rely on Him. What does it mean for the grace of God to be sufficient? How does it apply to my addiction to food and the process of overcoming obesity? What type of life am I afforded in lieu of my struggle?

I've learned along the way that we encounter the answers not simply from dialogue but through everyday life. This isn't simple book knowledge. To be honest, I grew up observing many people discuss the truth about God's power, but it was quite ironic to me because I never knew anyone to openly conquer obesity and food addiction.

I felt alone in the battle.

That image made it quite difficult for me to believe it was actually possible. In my own personal journey I've learned in order to truly know the power of God's grace and strength, a mere discussion will never do it justice. Some things you'll only know and understand from having a personal encounter with God.

The Gift of Grace

One day I decided to take a leap of faith—to step outside of my circumstances and into unknown territory. I took God up on his offer, and along the way, God has overwhelmed me with his sufficient grace and miraculous, life-altering strength.

The gift of grace is one of the greatest and most needed resources known to man. Grace in simple words is God's willingness to fill the gaps, providing in areas that we could not do so for ourselves. The more I realize my need for God, the more evident and present His grace is to come alongside me in my journey of life to fill the gaps and meet the need.

The areas in my life where I am deficient, God comes along and supplements my deficiencies with His abounding grace, and my experience with it strengthens me to face my battles in life and triumph. Thus, God continues to supply me with the tools necessary to deal with my addiction.

My addiction to food is my area of deficiency, and God came alongside me years ago and began supplying me with tactics and tools to defeat the beast. It's as if I am the biblical character David battling Goliath, and every day, God's grace is my slingshot, ready take out the beast that seeks to destroy me. Goliath didn't simply walk away. David had to show up to the battle against Goliath, and when on the scene, God influenced David to take a rock and a slingshot to destroy the giant. Likewise, God has given me rocks and slingshots that have assisted me in taking out my giant of food addiction, gluttony, and obesity. Every day I must show up to the battlefield with a winning mentality.

Overcoming is a Lifestyle

Anyone who struggles with an addiction can attest to the fact that conquering addiction requires you to realize that it is a lifestyle. It isn't a to-do item on a checklist you simply get to mark off and move on. There isn't a finish line per se. When you train, you train for a lifetime, as if a finish line doesn't exist. That's how you set yourself up to win and position yourself to use the tools God provides to fight.

To be honest, sometimes that truth can be very discouraging. Sometimes I want to simply move on to the next thing in life. One thing I've learned on this journey that helps keep me in the right perspective is the truth that victory over obesity happens one decision at a time.

Sometimes I get so focused on the tomorrow or ten years from now that I adopt a state of anxiety, worrying about whether I can handle or maintain the journey and the results.

However, one of the greatest lessons learned is that God is my daily strength. He gives me enough power to face my right now. Truth be told, all we need is power for the moment because we only face life one moment at a time. Winning the battle of addiction happens by exercising my faith daily.

Our lives lived in God are about our daily walk with Him. Your courage is built daily. Your perseverance is built daily. Your endurance and fortitude are built by making daily decisions. Longevity is made through the course of daily decisions. There is no such thing as an overnight arrival. Winning in the face of addiction is simple. It's not easy, but it is simple. You choose to show up and engage yourself, your deficiency, this world, and most importantly, God on a day-to-day, moment-by-moment basis. This is where you find your ultimate victory. Consider these truths:

- You are not defined by your previous decisions and are incapable of knowing the future, but you realize the present is always the most valuable time you have to make decisions that can consistently empower and transform you beyond what you thought possible. When you do, you begin to see yourself do and live in ways that were once unimaginable. Basically, you begin to encounter the wonderful grace of God at work in your life.

- You begin to envision yourself in greater ways than prior, which encourages you to continue to show up as an active participant in your own healing and freedom.

- Your mind, paradigm, and perspective of how you see yourself begins to shift. You start to live your life from an attitude that you are not your circumstance. They do not define you but rather give you an opportunity to overcome hardship.

- The true measure of who you are is seen in your triumph and not in your deficiency. You are humble enough to recognize your area of weakness, but you grow to have the audacity to believe your circumstances are merely a situation, positioned in such a way it produces growth and character in you. It develops compassion, empathy, and a heart to connect with the rest of broken humanity that surrounds you daily.

- You begin to identify life as an opportunity to be great rather than a roadblock from perfection. You begin to realize maybe life is not about becoming someone but rather about realizing you already are that someone and that you are simply coming to terms with acknowledging it as opposed to creating it. God doesn't want your faith in something in the making. He wants you to put your faith in something already made.

The Issue of Disbelief

I now realize I was always able to conquer my obesity and food addiction. I was hindered by my own disbelief. I didn't believe I had enough power inside of me to actually counteract that powerful desire to eat what I wanted when I wanted and whatever amount I desired. I fed into the lie that difficult equates to impossible. One reason many people don't overcome their addiction is because they simply don't believe they can. They continue to lose the battle because they don't actually think it's an option to win.

I believed losing my weight was really hard, which perhaps translated to impossible. Over time, I came to realize winning takes practice—an intentional decision to not stop at failure but to continue to try. It takes practice, consistency, determination, and endurance. The more times you decide to show up and engage with a determination to win, your odds of actually winning are increased.

I remember sitting at a meal with some friends. It was a buffet-style breakfast the church had provided for us after a service. The lady next to me looked at my plate and said, "You make it seem so easy." She was referring to fact that the food options on my plate were healthier and not full of fat and sugar.

I replied, "What makes you say that?"

She replied, "Look at my plate and look at your plate."

I turned to her and replied, "It's not easy at all. I just do it."

Culture and circumstances around us have caused us to believe the lie that if it doesn't come natural or with ease, then it's just too difficult to obtain. There is a belief that flourishing in a particular area is typically marked by one's natural ability to do well at it. I beg to differ. My life is an example that there are other ways in which a person can do exceptionally well at something. The key is honesty and consistency.

Insatiable Flesh

One day I was sitting in Bible study at my church. It was a regular Tuesday night, and the leader said something that forever changed my life. "The flesh is insatiable." I'm sure I'd heard it said before, but that specific night changed my life. Over and over people have heard me say, "God has been my strength on this journey." It's so real, yet often very difficult to perfectly describe how He manages to do just that.

One way in which He has been my strength is that he inserts at the right time what I need to push past a particular struggle that I might be facing or gives insight that causes me to contemplate, dig deep, search my own heart, and make a choice to move forward.

Well, this particular night really helped me gain insight on my relationship with food and whether I would actually continue to conquer or not. I recall being in a place in my journey where I just felt a little overwhelmed. I had lost more than 150 pounds by this point, and while most people were praising my efforts, they hardly knew the depths of the struggle and the reality of my everyday fight. Then, in the middle of the Bible study, the leader said, "The flesh is insatiable."

I don't even fully remember what we were talking about, but as clear as day, those words stood out to me, *the flesh is insatiable.* It was as if God was speaking directly to me. No one knew the thoughts or the struggles I was facing at that time, and I was sure God was trying to get my attention because those four words pierced my heart deeply.

God was trying to reveal something to me that was essential in me moving forward. It dawned on me in that moment, my body was never going to tell me no. There was never going to be a point where my body was going to reject the food and stop me from going overboard. It wasn't going to overtake my decision and choose for me. It wasn't going to necessarily make this thing easy for me and simply stop desiring the food.

For me it is food and for someone else it may be sex, porn, shopping, or stealing. The point is, our flesh—our desires—are insatiable. There is not a point of satisfaction where my body doesn't want more and more. Think about it: this is why they call marijuana a gateway drug. You're only going to want more because our flesh is never satisfied.

The truth was that the hardest and yet most powerful decision I would have to constantly make was going to be a daily decision to tell myself, "Enough. No more!" I was going to have to continue to be in the driver's seat and be intentional about cultivating the art of self-denial.

And to be completely honest, that scares me. I often feel so weak, incapable, defeated, and to think that the power to win the battle against obesity lies within my own decisions is extremely scary. I don't know a more honest way to put it, and yet, after losing so much weight, I can honestly say, the more aware I am of my weakness, the stronger I am because I am able to equip myself to fight.

Learning to tell yourself no isn't easy. It takes practice and consistency. Ultimately, you are training your mind to acknowledge that all your decisions in life should not be driven by pure desire. For example, when I eat pizza, I usually want more than the two slices that I ought to eat. In the past, I would go back for several servings, even though I was no longer hungry. When I began my weight loss journey I recognized my pattern and I instituted the practice of self-talk. I say things like, "Liana, if you go back for more pizza, you will regret it in the morning." Sometimes it worked and sometimes it didn't but the more I conversed with myself, overtime the will to resist strengthened and learning to tell myself no became easier. Your mind is like a muscle that has to be developed and strengthened. For example, I didn't start off doing one hundred pushups. There was a day I could only do three, and I just kept doing them every day, and as I continued to do them, my ability increased. My upper body strength grew and thus, I was able to produce more pushups.

Willpower works the same way. You have to continue in a

particular direction over the course of time, and as you strengthen your mind daily, the ability to resist and gain decision-making power only increases. This only happens with practice and consistency.

The problem is most people quit before they give themselves the opportunity to grow and engage in the process. When it gets tough, the desire to give in begins to overshadow the reason why most people decided to engage in the fight in the first place. I have said before, your why has to be strong enough to keep you on the journey. You have to remind yourself as much as necessary of the reason why you must deny and master your insatiable flesh.

What is your why? Why are you reading this book? What do you need to surrender to God but you don't because you are afraid you can't go the distance? What are you addicted to but you desperately want the power to overcome? For me, it is food and gluttony. What is it for you? What is robbing you of the joy of experiencing the fullness of today? Once you identify what it is, then you can begin to move forward.

I've had to come to terms with the reality that I have an addiction to food. It's not the end of my story, but if I'm ever going to defeat my enemy, I have to first be able to identify it. Living in the truth has set me free in ways that have been unimaginable. Here is one of my blog entries from July 9, 2011, which was a result of an aha moment I had surrounding my insatiable flesh and the potential impact of my decisions:

MY EPIPHANY ABOUT FOOD AND FEELINGS

I realize I eat/ate so much because I really enjoy the taste of food, and I get large amounts of food because I don't want that taste to cease, but the reality of it is that it will cease. There will come a moment I am no longer eating that dish. So the question becomes not if the moment will cease but when will the moment cease. And more so, after that moment has ceased, how do I feel? What are the lasting results of my decision? For example, I can eat one cookie or the entire bag, but at some point I will no longer be eating the cookie, and how will I feel about myself and how will my body be impacted after I make the decision?

If I eat one cookie, I would have enjoyed the taste of the cookie, I will feel good about myself, and I would not have gained weight/unhealthy side effects. Or, I can eat the whole bag, enjoy the taste, feel extremely guilty and down about myself, and my body would have been negatively impacted.

I know my thought process on food is extensive, but it's what it takes to help me make good decisions.

One Decision at a Time

My realization was simple yet profound. I was able to identify a truth, and once I knew it, I had to make a decision about what I was going to do with what I had come to realize. The more aware I am of how deeply impacted I am by my addiction, the more I realize in my own power I don't have all the tools to fight.

My addiction consistently requires me to rely on God as my strength. I often feel very weak and unable to control my desires to the point where it is completely overwhelming. And beyond that, it is often difficult for me to share my struggle because I feel ashamed or embarrassed about my reality. I feel like people's responses would be, "It's just food!" I wish that were the case. I wish I could handle food in a manner where it does not have the impact on my life that it does. Trust me, life would be so much easier. However, that is not my story.

So, one way I fight to stay on top is I have a personal declaration. It is one of my life's mottos: "Victory over obesity…one decision at a time." Sometimes people say, "One day at a time." And I respond, "Even a day can seem overwhelming and impossible." I take my life, one decision at a time. I choose to trust God moment by moment, allow the past to motivate me to keep going and leave the future where it belongs—in God's hands.

God Down the Road

I was sitting in a leadership team meeting at church one day, and my mentor, Dr. LaBeach, was leading. She opened up our time together by telling a story about her life and how years ago she auditioned to go on tour for the famous musical, *Rent.* She was in the middle of a graduate program at the time, and her life was already moving in a particular direction.

However, she made it clear to God that if she received the part in the musical, she would leave life as she knew it and jump on board to embark on this tour and possible life-altering opportunity. She was extremely excited about it and was pretty much ready to leave all else behind and just go for it. In the middle of waiting and preparation for what might be, she prayed a simple yet powerful prayer to God: "If you don't want me to go on this tour, don't let her call me back because if she calls, I am going." My mentor never heard back. She continued on with life as she knew it, and years later she found herself walking through the auditorium where she first auditioned for her part, wondering if that was supposed to be her life and if she had possibly missed out on the opportunity of a lifetime.

While walking through the auditorium, she ran into the lady who had auditioned her years prior. She asked the lady if she remembered her, and over the course of the conversation, the lady told her, "You made the right decision. You are on the right course, and you took the right route. You are doing what you were created to do."

By their miniature interaction, this lady was confident my mentor was living and thriving in her element. My mentor is a doctor—a psychologist—and has impacted so many lives, especially mine, and if she had gone on that tour, she would not be the woman she is—on the path she is on today, impacting lives like she does right now. In that moment, Dr. LaBeach encouraged and affirmed us all by reminding us God is in the "not yet," awaiting your arrival.

In God's economy, He sees fairness very differently than we do. Our perspective is so limiting, and I struggle with that daily. However, my trust in God is stronger than my struggles with uncertainty and doubt. I am not saying I don't often walk around with confusion or a lack of understanding, but what I am saying is it fails in comparison to the faithfulness of an all-knowing God. My mentor could have been upset with God for not receiving the role, and I can be upset with God for allowing me to struggle with my addiction with food.

Real talk? It often feels very unfair. However, in the midst of my doubt and frustration, I choose to constantly hand it over to God. I don't think it's fair that I have an addiction that I can't snap my fingers and make go away. I will probably never have an extremely fast metabolism and be able to eat whatever I want like my friends. I realize we all have something. My something may be food while someone else struggles with schizophrenia and the girl down the street was born blind. All I am saying is everyone has something. Now, what you do with your something and how you manage it in order to live a victorious life is a journey you walk out daily with God.

If God never removes my struggle with food, He will surely give me the strength to continuously overcome. What I've found to be even more incredible is that my struggle has not been in vain. The mere fact that you are reading this book right now is evidence that my story has value. Something good—no, great—has been produced out of my pain and suffering, and greatness will come out of yours as well.

Just as in the story of my mentor, I would not be the girl I am today if I did not walk through life's storms, and to be honest, I kind of like me. I absolutely love the person I am today. Trust me, I'm not saying I enjoyed or would want to ever relive or offer anyone what I went through. However, God saw my today, and He knew the process wasn't simply the process, but rather it had a purpose. My pain wasn't wasted. It had purpose, and my story is still being written.

Has my addiction to food ceased? No! But my perspective on the value of my life and how I'm willing to fight for it has completely been altered. Now I see my weakness isn't the end of my story, and choosing not to fight only makes life more miserable and less joyous. It's not going to be my way. I have to make choices—hard but necessary choices.

We are all dealt a deck of cards, but we have so much power in how we play the game. See, God knew my life before I was even born. He was in my future while He was at the same time carrying me through my present. That's how dope God is. We can only see our present state, and we don't even have the full perspective of it. God has a panoramic view of our lives. Trust me, it is not a coincidence that you are reading this book, this chapter, this page, these particular words right now. There is a lesson to be learned, some insight to be gained, power to be accessed, and a life full of victory to be lived.

God introduced you to my story so it would propel you to hope again, believe again, dream again, and dare to take a step of faith out of your circumstances into the beauty of the unknown where a more than capable and extremely faithful God resides. No, you can't have it all and your flesh may be insatiable, but what you do have is the power to choose. So make a choice to stop simply existing and start living.

Realizing Grace

God gives us tools—grace—to win in the face of addiction. He has helped me realize some key elements that have truly helped me conquer and continue to conquer. I typically refer to these as aha moments. They are moments of revelation. It's like the lightbulb comes on and I gain new and fresh insight into tactics that work for me. Not everything works for everybody, but the following areas have been very integral to my continual well-being in the face of this beast of an addiction:

Realize that overcoming is a lifestyle. The realization that choosing not to give in to gluttony is not a one-time event or a special season in life that will just go away. It is much more likely that this is the order of my life. I have to position myself to see my struggle as an area I have to position myself to face on an ongoing basis. This is not a sprint but perhaps more like a marathon. Therefore, it's not about making extreme decisions that are not sustainable. It's about learning yourself and making the choices that will propel you to live well in the face of your struggle. I had to learn my addiction is something I will most likely face every day, and if that's the case, like anything else that matters to me, I prepare to acknowledge it and I go the distance to tackle it head-on. I've had to learn what environments are healthy and not so healthy for me, what people encourage my victory, and which people hinder my success. It's all about doing what it takes to live the lifestyle appropriate to ensuring your ongoing success.

Victory takes place one decision at a time. Anxiety is not my friend. It causes me to shut down and exist in an ongoing state of fear and uncertainty. I only live one moment at a time. That's all I have to worry about. Life is about making the next decision. The past doesn't define me, and the future is yet to come, but one thing I do know is my greatest ability is when I choose to take ownership of the moment. As I continue to take control of the moment and choose victory in my right now, I look up, and as time has passed, all those individual moments add up. You will never lose one hundred pounds until you lose five pounds, and the only way you lose five pounds is by making the necessary decisions in each moment to do so. That method of thinking helps me to realize that every decision matters, and no one decision is too small or insignificant. Maximizing on the moment has been my greatest strength and has produced my greatest reward.

I have to choose to show up every day. You get better at the things you practice. It is as simple as that. I had to practice telling myself no. The more I tell myself no, the stronger I become in my ability to do so. Courage is not built overnight. Resistance doesn't happen in a moment. Defeat takes time, intentionality, and consistency. I have to choose to be present in the affairs of my own life. Overcoming gluttony and being healthy is strengthened like every other area of my life, by choosing to prioritize the practice of it. If I mess up, I get back up, and I try again because eventually, the more I practice, my likelihood of failing decreases. How do I know? It took me four years, but I lost the excess weight. I chose to practice and practice until I learned how to master my flesh. It's tough, but it works, and life without it is not living. It's simply existing.

I vow to be honest with myself. The lie we often tell ourselves is "I don't care." I realize this one little lie keeps many people stuck. We do care. We often feel helpless and incapable, but we care. Choosing to be honest with yourself exposes the areas in which you can seek help and assistance. However, we often lie because the truth feels shameful. We don't give ourselves credit to feel like it's okay to feel weak, vulnerable, fragile, and helpless.

We think it's pitiful to feel this way, and thus we ignore it and suppress the truth, which encourages the pattern of self-defeat. Facing the truth gives you the courage to seek help.

The gift of self-talk. I talk to myself all the time. I evaluate my life and my difficulties. I say things to myself like, "Liana, if you quit, you are not going to be happy. Giving up is not going to produce the results you want. It may be difficult, but you must continue because if you don't you'll be even more unhappy later on. Quitting right now won't give you want you want." Self-talk really helps me to examine my life and make choices beyond my temporary, momentary circumstances.

These have been lessons learned. They have really transformed my approach to facing my addiction. Aha moments are really powerful. I thank God for being my grace, filling the gap, and being my strength in my area of deepest need. He is extending the invitation to do the same for you. Remember to be encouraged. You are embarking on something most people never will, and it's for one simple reason: they don't believe they can. From one addict to another: you can do this. Calm down, relax, breathe, and remember your deficiency is not a hindrance to your success but an opportunity for God to give you the strength to overcome and live victoriously. The question isn't what you're able to do but rather, what you're willing to submit yourself to doing.

Can't Have it All

Burger King had a motto "Have it Your Way..." and it has saturated our mindset. We live in a culture that tells us we can have what we want, when we want it just the way that we want it. Oh, how I desperately wish that were true because it would make my life so much easier.

For a girl like me, who has a deep love for food and an immense desire to always look and feel good, there remains a tension between both realities. I mean really, struggling with obesity and food addiction for the majority of my life has been no joke. For example, right now it's 10:00 P.M. and as I sit here and write this book, I am oh so desiring to go eat a nice big slice of carrot cake. And the internal battle that I face makes it very plain and clear, I can't have it all. If I could have it all and have it my way, the internal struggle would not even exist; there would be no battle in my mind. Rather than getting carrot cake, I am still writing because of a valuable lesson I have learned: Some benefits come as a result of self-discipline and denying my flesh its immediate gratification.

Why do I say this? Unfortunately, life is full of choices, and with every choice comes *sacrifice*. No one likes the word sacrifice. I surely don't. But 180 pounds later, I must say, I have learned along this journey I must tell myself no in order to tell myself yes. I can't eat an entire box of pizza and still wear those skinny jeans I love to fit into. This is much easier said than done. The reality I had to embrace is that the moment isn't everything. The immediate desire often feels like it's everything, and all that matters is satisfying the flesh right then and there, but that sort of limited vision will never get me where I want to be. Self-discipline is so hard, but the results are so worth it. It is the road less traveled but the one with great reward.

Perhaps, like me, you have friends who are extremely skinny, can eat what they want, and never gain a pound. That is not my story. Seriously, my best friend from childhood weighed like one hundred pounds, and she can eat for days and never gain a pound. Another one of my closest friends eats Big Macs from McDonald's like they are carrot sticks, and all I can think of is how lucky I think they are.

Sure, we know it's about more than just looking good. Internal health is a priority. It doesn't make me feel any happier that my body isn't wired in such a manner that I can go eat my carrot cake and be carefree about it. Even in the midst of what seems unfair, I have options. I can sit around and continuously envy my friends' reality, or I can accept the truth. We were made differently, and following their lifestyle will never allow me to reach my goals. To live as they live will inevitably set me up for failure. I would have never lost the weight if I sat around comparing myself to what seemed to me as unfair circumstances. I had a choice, and I still have choices that require me to be particular about setting myself up to win. Time after time, I have had to coach myself and talk to myself and force myself to push past apathy and discouragement because ultimately, it is worth it.

Ironically, I am sitting here writing this chapter, Tuesday, November 6, 2012, after President Obama just won his second term as the president of the United States of America. And I promise you, his road to presidency, much like my fight to gain victory over obesity came with many sacrifices along the way. Greatness costs you something. Living well costs you something. Honestly, every single decision you ever make in your life will cost you something, and the sooner you realize that, the clearer the path becomes.

The question no longer becomes if you will sacrifice but rather what will you sacrifice. What are you willing to give up—to relinquish—in order to position yourself to gain? Is there something even greater you seek to gain? The answers to those questions will determine the choices you make in your life from here on out. When you've decided your priorities and set your mind on achieving them, it legitimatizes everything else you'll be required to let go of.

CHAPTER 6

THE BEAST CALLED DISCOURAGEMENT

My story is not one where I can say it's been completely smooth or without difficulty. I wish I could say I've never had a setback or a moment of discouragement, but that just isn't the reality of my life. I've had some really hard hitters—days when I've said, "Forget it. It's not worth it." There have been days when I sat in my room and cried because of doubt, fear, and fatigue. I have had those moments where I felt too mentally weak to continue or the thought of doing this thing forever just simply felt way too overwhelming. Imagine losing one hundred pounds and still being obese. That can be pretty discouraging!

Between 2007 and 2008, I had lost one hundred pounds. Let that sink in for a moment. On my own, I lost it all. The girl who was convinced she couldn't lose five pounds in one year had lost pretty much what my best friend weighed. That was such an amazing accomplishment. It was huge for me. I had never been more proud of myself. Victory never tasted so sweet. One hundred pounds, are you kidding me? A lot of prayer, hard work, and dedication created the path to my success. I faced that mountain in my life called obesity. I was on an all-time high.

The year 2008 was the absolute best one of my life. But then, a change occurred. A shift took place. It wasn't all roses and candy. Reality hit, and it hit hard.

Reality Sets In

After losing one hundred pounds, I was happy, but I was also very tired. The reality of my condition began to overshadow my victory. I had lost so much weight and I was still obese. Who loses one hundred pounds and steps on the scale obese? The thought of that drained me. Thoughts of shame and frustration started to overwhelm me. How did I let myself get that big? Why didn't I stop overeating earlier? What had I allowed my life to become? I began to focus more on the fact that I was still overweight and the thought that I still had about one hundred pounds left to lose. My discouragement grew. I had come so far, yet I had so far left to go.

The year 2009 was a very difficult one. I started to plateau. I wasn't dropping weight at the same rate I was the previous year. I began to slip up on some of my eating habits. I was still active, but I knew I wasn't as committed as I previously was. I was tired. I just wanted a break in life. I wanted to not have to work so hard to get the results I wanted. In my mind, I wanted to be like everyone else. For the majority of my life I had felt like others had the privilege to engage food in a way I didn't, and it just didn't seem fair. I wanted to be able to eat how I wanted versus how I needed to eat and still get my desired results, but it just wasn't happening that way.

For goodness' sake, after losing one hundred pounds you would think God would cut me some slack, speed this metabolism up or something. All of 2009 went by, and this reality seemed to be my consistent battle. I would gain weight then lose it. I was trying to just find a pace again and balance it with the reality of my frustrations.

By December 2009, my body had changed some because I was still working out, but I had not lost any significant weight, and it was tough. After coming so far, I felt defeated. Who feels defeated after losing one hundred pounds? For me, the answer was a girl who was more focused on how far she had left to go rather than how far she had already come.

However, I knew going backward wasn't an option.

On New Year's Eve 2009, I resolved that in 2010, I would get back on track and figure out what I needed to do to continue strong on the journey I had begun. I had recommitted my resolve to moving forward and to do what it would take to gain a victorious life. The year 2010 was about to be my year. Watch out. I just knew once I entered the new year everything would shift in my mind and I would be set to go.

The Monday Mentality

Think about how we treat January 1, like it is oh so miraculous. It is as if some supernatural shift takes place that forces us to do right when the new year comes. I call that the Monday mentality, which is putting off until tomorrow what desperately needs to be done today. It's as if all of a sudden, everything that was wrong will just snap into place and become right.

As much as we convince ourselves this is the case, we all know from experience there is nothing miraculous about January 1. In and of itself it's simply just another day—if you allow it to be.

The shift never ever takes place in time; it always takes place in your mind.

There's nothing different about yesterday or today or tomorrow if nothing changes inside of us. Think about it. Years had passed before without me losing any weight. What was different about the year I lost one hundred pounds and the previous years I hadn't lost any weight? It wasn't that 2008 was supernatural or out of the ordinary, as far as time is concerned. It was that a shift took place inside of me. I discovered a reason to live and to live well.

My Big Break

To think the year 2010 would simply turn the switch back on was foolish on my behalf. I knew better than that. I had come too far to slip back into old thinking patterns, but that's what happens when a person grows discouraged and allows doubt and fear to slip back in to the picture. I went into 2010, and before I knew it, it was already March and I hadn't lost any weight. I had set a resolution, and still, I couldn't seem to find my footing. I desperately wanted to continue in a conquering pattern, but I hovered in a place of discouragement.

People would say to me, "Liana, you have come so far. You've already lost one hundred pounds. You can do this."

I was like, "Exactly. I've lost one hundred pounds. Do you

know what it took? All the sweat, tears, discipline, commitment, sacrifice, self-denial, planning, and preparation that it took to bring me this far?"

The thought that I would have to put that much or more effort in to see myself the rest of the way was simply overwhelming. I was already three months into the new year, and my resolution was not panning out the way I had hoped it would.

Then, out of nowhere, my goddaughter's mother called me and told me the show *The Biggest Loser* was coming to Los Angeles and that I should audition.

I figured, this had to be it. I'd lost 100 pounds on my own, and God was bringing *The Biggest Loser* my way to help me go the distance, to finish strong. Right in my time of need, I felt as if God was delivering my big break. He was honoring my hard work and was about to afford me the opportunity of a lifetime. I was very excited—a little nervous but more so excited because I felt like my prayer was finally being answered.

The audition was early on a Saturday morning. I woke up while it was still dark, drove to the Citadel Outlets and was in line by 5:00 A.M. There were so many people out there. Everyone was in line waiting for their chance to finally get their opportunity of a lifetime. Everyone seemed so desperate to finally escape the bondage of their obesity, and deep inside my heart was aching.

I was in a line full of people who felt hopeless and desperate for *The Biggest Loser* to change their lives. Many were convinced if they didn't get this opportunity, they had no clue as to how they would move forward. I had this conflict in my heart. I wanted it for myself, but I wanted it for them too. My heart flooded with emotions as I saw people who could barely walk or even breathe. Here I was, probably the most athletic of them all, just as desperate for this chance. It felt like my only hope, but in reality I had already shown myself I could do this without the show.

However, I would not even let that thought have much room in my mind. I was in this line, and I was certain I was about to shine in my interview, and my opportunity was waiting for me on the other side of this audition.

The Audition Process

The interview went quickly. It was actually a group interview. They took about ten to twelve of us at a time, and we had about five to ten minutes to make our mark. It was quite nerve racking, but I didn't let it stop me. I did what I could to stand out but also remain authentic to who I was.

While I am an extremely sociable person, I'm not

necessarily the girl who's automatically extroverted, regardless of the surroundings. It takes me a minute to feel out the territory and find my place in a setting. On this occasion, I didn't have that luxury. Time was of the essence, and I needed to make my mark—and make it quick. I thought I did pretty well. I was confident, passionate, sweet, and sincere. I was Liana in a snapshot. I remember walking away thinking, *This is my time.* The next step was for me to go home and make an at-home audition video and turn it in.

Now, the tricky part. Though people in my life had witnessed me losing weight, I was not extremely vocal about the process. If you were in my life, you knew in what I was engaging, but I didn't expose myself to the world. I hadn't publically revealed what was taking place, so to have to make this video was quite a step in the direction of transparency and vulnerability.

I would have to share why I needed the show and why it needed me. I had to go deep to the degree I had to expose parts of my body that were uncomfortable to reveal. I was willing to be extremely open and transparent because I truly wanted this opportunity.

For the first time in my life, I exposed my half naked body on film. I felt ashamed and very helpless, but I knew it was now or never. With great confidence, I sent my video off. I even posted it on Facebook and started sharing it with people in my life. Everyone was encouraging and confident my video was a winner. For the first time in a long while, my hope factor was real.

The Thing About Hope

When I was a kid, I had a lot of dreams for myself. But somewhere I stopped hoping. What do I mean? Hope means a confident expectation. Many times people use the word, but what they really mean is *wish*. Hope entails confidence while what people often mean is "I wish…it would be nice if it occurred." Somewhere along the line, I had lost my confidence. I stopped believing exceptionally good things would occur for me. I wished they would, but I no longer expected them to because I lacked confidence. I didn't believe my name would be called or my number would be pulled and that life would just bring a big break my way, so I started wishing and left hope in the past. I would use the word, but not with its true intention or meaning.

For the first time in a really long while I actually hoped again. I didn't know if I would actually make the show, but I believed I would. I had a confidence that felt so real you couldn't convince me this wasn't God's special gift tailor made for me.

The timing was impeccable. I had been praying something special would occur to get me back on track, and before you knew it, *The Biggest Loser* was in town, and I was certain this was it.

Anxiety grew as time passed and I didn't hear from the show. The beginning of the season was nearing and I hadn't heard a word. I checked my email nonstop and nothing new had come through. They didn't send signs of acceptance or rejection. Nothing! At this point, I just wanted to know, and there was not a sound around town about whether I had made the show.

My hope began to turn into fear and thoughts of torment. I was sure if I didn't make the show I would be devastated, broken, and left wondering what I would do with my life. I would be crushed, not just because I didn't make the show but more so because I gave God a huge piece of my heart. I hoped again. I actually believed He would deliver something great on my behalf.

Let me explain something. Not a day in my life goes by where I doubt God's ability to perform. My greatest area of faith was in His willingness to perform on my behalf. I know God can do anything, but what God *can* do and what He will do are not synonymous. So to believe God's ability and His willingness were actually about to align in my life in a way that meant so much to me was epic.

But as time passed, fear *The Biggest Loser* wouldn't happen increased and my disappointment in the thought He would let me down in this great season of hope was overwhelming. Like, really God? You want me to hope, right? So if you want me to hope, would you really not deliver? Don't you want my faith to increase? If you give me the show, all it would do is grow my faith and belief factor. Then, I can tell everyone what you did for me, then others will trust you too. What a win-win situation.

At least that is what I thought.

Shattered Hope

I never did hear from the show, not a word. They didn't send an acceptance or a rejection. They just left me hanging. The way I found out I didn't make it was when I was invited to be a part of the taping of the first episode. They were hosting a city-wide exercise challenge on the beach as part of the season premiere. By being invited to the exercise challenge for the city, I realized they had chosen who the contestants were for the show and it was not me. I was invited simply to be part of a larger audience. When I received that invite, I melted. I cried and cried. My heart was so heavy and I was in a place of deep despair. Not only did I not receive my chance of a lifetime, but I actually hoped again and the disappointment I experienced felt like the worst thing ever. I put my heart on the line and God didn't protect it. At least, that's how I felt.

God knew how fragile and vulnerable I was, and He didn't take care of me in my time of need. A part of me knew my journey wasn't over, but another part of me felt too defeated to get back up and try again. The thought of the amount of effort it would take to finish strong was tiring in and of itself.

Have you ever been tired just thinking about what you have to do? Consider your long list of action items and that can make you tired in and of itself. Well, that was how I felt thinking about engaging in the next chapter of my weight-loss story. I was tired and discouraged. I was sad and frustrated with God. The one person I was supposed to be able to depend on left me to fend for myself. It was like time had frozen, and I was paralyzed by fear and pain. I wanted that opportunity so bad I could taste it, and God said no. What do you do when God says no? That was the reality I was faced with, and it just didn't seem fair.

One day I was in my living room, and I was just sad that I hoped again and it was unfulfilled. But something happened while I was sitting on the floor. My computer went into sleep mode, and images of my weight-loss journey began to go across the screen. The vision of these images was as if God was trying to communicate with me. In the midst of all of the pain and discouragement, it was as if a soft peace came over me. Out of nowhere, an unusual sense of confidence and hope began to penetrate my heart. The thought came to my mind, *God has brought me this far without a show...He can surely take me the rest of the way.*

In the middle of suffering, God whispered hope into my situation. "Do you trust me to take you all the way, Liana?" That was God's challenge to me. "Do you really believe I brought you this far to leave you obese? Is that the kind of God you think I am?"

I was so concerned about the method in which I wanted God to help me that I didn't stop long enough to realize my hope should have never been placed in the opportunity of the show.

God was writing a story with my life I had no idea of. It wasn't wrong for me to hope again. However, my hope was misplaced. My faith was in what I wanted God to do for me instead of in God alone. When you place your hope in God alone, you worry less about the method, and you focus on the God who is able to make a way out of what appears to be an impossible set of circumstances. God told me no because it wasn't best for me. There was something He was trying to show me that required me to get passed my sorrow and focus on what was next.

I am so glad He told me no, but I didn't realize the no was good then. I had to let go of my disappointment in order to move forward. I once heard a very wise woman say, "God is in your tomorrow awaiting your arrival."

My life is a testament to this fact. I can only see my life right now and even in that, I have a limited perspective. However, the road ahead of me has already been paved, and it's simply my duty to walk the path one step at a time, relying on faith in God to guide each step of the journey.

Restoration Through Discouragement

Even though I didn't make the show, I decided to go ahead and attend the season premiere, and I participated in the city-wide exercise challenge of which I was invited to be a part. That day, I committed to re-engage my journey. Standing at the beach with a friend of mine, I created *WatchQueenLose.blogspot.com* right then and there.

I decided I would create a blog that would welcome others into my journey. It would be a source of accountability for me. Over time it has become as source of strength and encouragement for so many people who struggle just like I do. I didn't have an example, but finally I was becoming that example for others. I was going to be living proof obesity could be conquered one day at a time and one decision at a time.

Every week I would check in and share updates, my goals, my eating regimen, and my thoughts about the process. I would just lay it all out there. I started my YouTube channel, *TheQueenLiana*, as well, and I would post video updates every single Tuesday without fail.

On June 1, 2010, I began publically sharing my journey with the world. I didn't expose myself on *The Biggest Loser* audition video the way I did simply to shrink back into a place of self-pity. The video was the first time I opened myself up to so many people, and it was a vehicle that allowed me to be vulnerable and transparent in a way I never had in my life.

I literally stripped myself before thousands because I needed something so badly I was willing to put my pride behind me. It was the beginning of something great, and I had no idea. Was it God's will for me to audition for the show? Yes. But it was never in His plan to give me the show.

God had a much bigger plan for me. Being denied by *The Biggest Loser* was an essential asset to my story. It was a necessary part of my story, though I didn't see it that way at the time. I now realize there was a bigger picture at play. God was not exclusively focused on my immediate circumstances. Giving me *The Biggest Loser* would have been a quick fix, but it would not have told the story God wanted my life to tell.

There were many lessons learned out of that experience:

1. I'm so much stronger than I thought. I always felt like I was weak and incapable of doing the extraordinary. I felt basic and average. God wanted to show me I didn't need a big break, that I could wake up every single day and fight to prove to myself that engaging the daily battle was worth it for the sake of my own personal freedom. Since not making the show, I have lost eighty more pounds, which brings me to a total of 180 pounds lost naturally. I still can't believe that is my story.

2. If I made the show, my life would not be a testimony to so many people like it is today. Most people will never have a trainer like Bob Harper or Jillian Michaels to work them out several hours a day. They will never be able to leave their daily routine of life and live on a ranch devoted to their weight-loss success. Most people will have to wake up every morning and decide whether they will prioritize their life in such a manner that makes health and fitness a priority. They will have to intentionally organize their life in a fashion that creates an opportunity for them to be

successful right at home. For many people, my story will be the first in which they've ever engaged where a person fought obesity at home without any extreme measures involved but rather a daily commitment to see it through.

3. Conquering obesity has increased my faith. I was the girl who thought I couldn't lose five pounds. Now that I've conquered what seemed impossible, impossible no longer exists to me. I have the audacity to believe I can do anything.

    The mere fact that I am sitting here writing this book is because I now believe in myself. The audacity to believe I can write a book worth reading that will make a mark on the world has come out of seeing myself conquering obesity. Walking this journey out day by day over the course of four years has increased my hope factor. It has spilled over into other areas of my life. When you conquer in one area, it starts to impact every other area because your mind is shifting and not just relegated to one area of your life. It begins to impact the overall person you are. Now, I believe I can do things that may not come naturally easy for me, but I still go after them because I now know I can excel in the face of difficulty.

    For example, I'm learning to play the acoustic guitar. In the past, I gave up because it was too hard, but now I realize if

I want something, I can't depend on it coming easy or naturally for me in order to engage in it. If I want it bad enough, my want has to supersede how challenging it may be, and my belief that I can do anything empowers me to keep showing up and working hard at it until I see and experience the desired result.

My Charge to You

What in your life seems like the end of the road? What didn't occur that you really wanted to happen and now you have lost your sense of hope? Are you stuck in what seems like failure or a missed opportunity? I encourage you to use my story as an example that it's only the end of the story if you allow it to be.

You can't see the full picture, and if you focus on your immediate circumstances, you're missing an opportunity to excel right now. Allow your setbacks or disappointments to propel you. Trust in God and not in what you expect His methods to be.

Allow my journey to inspire you to hope again, believe again, try again, and trust again. Live today and stop putting your life off. Leave your Monday mentality behind because I promise you, Monday will never come. Don't put off for tomorrow what desperately needs to happen today.

God can handle your disappointments. Just don't wallow in them. He appreciates your honesty and gives you room to vent, but in the midst of your venting, give God room to show you your story isn't finished being written. Take it from me, God wants to upstage your expectations of Him and bless you beyond that, then He'll turn around and use your life to encourage others. Don't quit.

CHAPTER 7

THE SURRENDER

Sometimes in life we get so overwhelmed by what we can't do and by the things we can't control that we lose sight of the power we have in what we can actually achieve.

Personally, I'm a bit of a control freak. I often lack patience, and I like things to be done my way and in my timing. When faced with situations I don't have control over, I get a bit antsy. I don't like sitting around and just waiting for time to unfold or for other people to do their part. I like to be in a position where I can ensure things pan out the way I would like. In so many words, I fool myself.

A False Sense of Control

I say I fool myself because if I slow down long enough to actually evaluate reality for what it is, I would realize there is very little I have control over. I don't determine when the sun rises or sets. I have no control over which mornings I will wake up, when my heart will start beating, or when my eyes will actually open. When I leave the house to go to work in the morning, I have no say over whether it will be the day I have or avoid a car accident. I'm not quite sure the next time I get into my car, it won't simply blow up or that while walking down the street I won't be mugged. Who's to say the next time I log into my bank account online all my funds won't have been compromised and tampered with? All this to say, I often think I'm in control, but in reality I'm in control of very little.

This journey has taught me to relinquish control and pick up responsibility. God is in control, but He gives me areas of stewardship I'm to oversee and manage well. I've learned I have to shift my thinking. This journey has not been about controlling my own life per se, but rather about learning how to take responsibility for the life God has given me and to trust He will strengthen me with everything I need to be successful.

Many times on this journey I've found myself in situations where I felt my strength fail me. I can keep getting frustrated or I can learn the lesson. I had to shift my perspective because perspective is everything. The best form of living is in partnership with God, so in my weakest of circumstances or when I have simply done all that I can do, there is strength gained from knowing there's one who is stronger than I and who is actually ultimately in control.

Consider when I was very discouraged and disappointed I didn't make *The Biggest Loser.* I had two options. I could have stopped there, or I could trust even though the situation caused me to feel defeated God was not going to abandon me in my weakest moments. Instead, I got up and decided to trust Him when I couldn't see the path ahead of me. I allowed Him to work in the midst of what I couldn't imagine or see possible. I had a shift in my thinking. I decided to not allow my strength to count for everything. I could only do my part and trust God would do His. There is power in surrendering control and simply picking up my personal, human responsibility.

An Example of God's Grace

Take a look into one of my blog posts.

On Tuesday, March 6, 2012, I wrote this entry on my blog: During my appearance on NBC's Today Show, it was highlighted that God has been my strength during this four-year weight-loss process. While I've had to put the work and effort into the 180-plus pounds I've loss, I am completely aware God has been my source and my strength during this process. During recent interviews I have done, post-appearance, I've been asked, "How has God been your strength?" Initially it was very difficult for me to answer that question because, while I value the art of communication, there is a reality that the human language has its limitations on being able to fully communicate the realities of life. However, there is one major way of the many that God has been my strength during this process. I have come to realize deep in my heart and in my experience one undeniable truth: I'm a firm believer God orchestrates the affairs of your life in such a way that He inserts at the perfect time that which you need to hold on, to endure, to make it to the next level.

With that stated, let me share some insights on the consultation I had with an amazing plastic surgeon today and how I even got to this point. As many of you may know, I've struggled with weight and obesity the majority of my life, since elementary, and in 2007, at the age of twenty-one and a weight of 356 pounds, I decided to yield myself to God and the process of losing the weight. I wanted to be free, and I knew I had to do what seemed impossible to me.

Over the course of these four years, I have worked extremely hard, and my body has changed in remarkable ways. I'm grateful for how the elasticity in my skin has snapped back pretty well, but I've been left with excess skin and fat tissues no amount of exercise will remove. On December 31, 2011, I created a video blog expressing my desire for surgeons, TV shows, anyone to sponsor my surgery. I have put a lot of effort into this process and have endured through difficulty, but I'm a struggling college graduate with loans and barely enough money to provide for my necessities. I put my video out there, and I decided to leave the process in God's hands. Time went on, and I continued with my life. I had not heard any concrete feedback, and I didn't doubt, but there were still moments of fear and discouragement in this process. See, even though I just got back from New York from doing the Today Show, for some reason I started experiencing some fear in my heart in relation to my relationship to food and this weight-loss process. Many people wouldn't understand, but when you're addicted to food, this is a daily process. Yes, I have lost 180 plus pounds, but I still have my days where I feel overwhelmed by the tug food has on me. I beg God to shut off the desires that are ever present in my mind and body, and as much as I want Him to remove them, He hasn't, but what He has reminded me and continues to remind me is that His grace is sufficient, and in my weakness His strength is made perfect. He will give me all I need to conquer and be victorious over the enemy and over my addiction.

On Wednesday, February 23, 2012, I went out to dinner with one of my amazing mentors, Dr. LaBeach, and while we were conversing, fear and pain led me to tears. I didn't realize how much I was allowing myself to be tormented by the thoughts that my addiction would win and that I would gain the weight back. God knows I want my story to be that I was a success and not that I relapsed.

I want people to look at me and believe difficult is not impossible and that this thing can really be conquered. I want to endure until the end, but sometimes it just feels like I'm too weak to fight. I cried, and we talked. She encouraged, I cried some more, and I was just real with where I was in my process. The last thing I want people to think is that this thing is easy for me, but even more so, I want people to know just because something isn't easy, it doesn't mean you can just throw in the towel and quit.

I went home that night feeling a little encouraged but still working through the fear. But God.

Thursday, March 12, 2012, I woke up to the most amazing email ever. Please hear me and hear me clearly. God sees you. One of the greatest joys in my life is to just sit back and think long enough to conclude God sees me. I received an email from a remarkable woman, my angel, Debbie. The email stated:

Hello Liana,

My name is Debbie. I'm a registered nurse at Kaiser. I was so amazed by your story that I sent a request to Dr. Pousti, a well-known plastic surgeon in the San Diego area. Below is the information I forwarded to him. I also sent before and after pictures and a link to your YouTube/blog. Please give him a call at your earliest convenience. Also check out his website http://www.poustiplasticsurgery.com.

By this point, I was in tears. I had not even yet read the actual email she sent to Dr. Pousti. I was just honored by the fact someone cared enough to stop and selflessly share my story. I'm amazed by the beauty of the human spirit, the blessedness of connectedness— the power of love.

The email she sent him stated:

Hello Dr. Pousti,

My name is Debbie. I am a registered nurse at Kaiser. I have heard of your surgical procedures and makeovers in the San Diego area. One of my coworkers spoke highly of you, and I enjoyed seeing the transformation in all of your clients on your website. I also did a little research, checked your rating/ scores, and was very impressed. You are one of the best plastic surgeons in the country. Sometime in the distant future, maybe a year or so, hopefully we will meet for a little make-

over myself, but still working on me at the present— fifty pounds down and more to lose.

I was browsing around on Facebook, minding my own business and came across an amazing young lady. Her name is Liana. She's an in-debt college student from the Los Angeles area. This woman has lost over 180 pounds without surgery (four-year weight-loss regimen) and is looking for assistance to have excess skin removed. Take a look at her video, for more information. I truly hope you can help her.

She has also been a guest on the NBC Today Show. I think she may also bring in great publicity for your company. I do not know her personally, but I do admire her strong willpower and endurance.

Dr. Pousti then responded:

> *Dear Debbie,*
>
> *Thank you for the very nice email. I would be happy to see her in the office to see what we can do to help her. Do you know her personally? If so, please ask her to call the office to set up a consultation for her and I to meet.*

I look forward to it. Again, I appreciate your kind words and look forward to meeting you in the future. Have a wonderful weekend!

Tom Pousti, M.D.

I called the office that very day and set up an appointment, and within days, Dr. Pousti had emailed me personally. I had no idea how I was going to make it to San Diego. My car was not in shape to endure the drive, and on top of that, I don't do well taking drives alone. But once again, I didn't fret. I set up the appointment on faith, trusting God would make a way for me to make it to this consultation. Normally, a consultation fee is one hundred dollars, but they waived the fee. However, if I missed the consultation, they were going to charge me. I set up the appointment not knowing how I was going to get there, but I knew I didn't have one hundred dollars to waste and that God was going to get me there. Long story short, my sister and I swapped cars for the day and my mom was available to take the drive with me.

My visit with Dr. Pousti was nothing short of an amazing God thing. I really wish I could communicate with my words what my heart is bursting to share. I mean really, my eyes are filling with tears as I sit here and type this post. His staff was extremely personable and accommodating. They handled me so well, and once I met Dr. Pousti, I was fully convinced he was the man God placed in my life to make this surgery happen for me. I was blown away by him, and he was blown away by me. Beyond how remarkable his experience is, his heart and compassion is even greater. A man of his expertise and experience stopped by to see about little old me.

He said to me, "Liana, I have done thousands of surgeries, and over my years of practice you are on the top ten list of most inspiring people I have met."

What? Are you kidding me? This man has been in his field for more than twenty years. I was five years old when he started doing surgeries, and he walks in and tells me I inspire him. I refused to cry in that office, but wow, I felt so affirmed.

To top it all off, one of my greatest fears is that I would walk in there and he would tell me I have so much weight left to lose before I could be operated on. As I changed into my gown to be examined, I just didn't want to hear those words. I'd put so much effort in, the last thing I needed to hear was how much more weight I needed to lose. He took one look at my body and looked back at me and said, "You've done all that is humanly possible. You've done the hard work. At the most you have five to ten more pounds to lose but really, you've done all that is humanly possible to do."

I thought, *Isn't that all that God requires of us, to do only what is humanly possible?*

I wish I could go more in depth on how this entire process over the past four years of my life has had enormous spiritual implications. God has taught me so much about life lived in Him, through this process of losing weight.

After Dr. Pousti examined me, he sat down and spoke with me and stated, "I am going to do all that I can do to help you."

I said, "Dr. Pousti, what does that mean?"

He then explained the cost of this surgery was not all him, meaning the plastic surgeon is only one piece of the pie in this whole process when it comes to financial expenses. There were four major components to the financial process: the plastic surgeon (Dr. Pousti), the anesthesiologist, the medical facilities where the surgery was performed, and the medicine prescribed to manage the pain during recovery.

Dr. Pousti could only promise his portion, but he couldn't guarantee the rest. He had agreed to be an advocate for me and to share my story with the other parties in an attempt to help me out as much as possible.

It Actually Happened

Would you believe at the time of this writing, I am now sitting here two months post-surgery? On September 24, 2012, Dr. Pousti performed an extended tummy-tuck surgery on me and was able to get all parties on board. My surgery was completely free. In the back of my mind, I hear the words he said to me the first day he met me: *Liana, you have done all that is humanly possible.* Basically, I took responsibility for my own life.

No, I am not in control. I had no idea Debbie was going to send Dr. Pousti my story or that he would say yes. I had no clue when I made my video request that in less than a year, my request would have been honored. I had no idea I would come to love Dr. Pousti and his staff as if they were a new extension to my family.

When I decided to face my obesity, I didn't know I would be sitting here writing this book about how epic these years of my life have been. All I knew was I was trapped and I needed to be set free. And God used Dr. Pousti to teach me a valuable lesson. We are only called to do what is humanly possible. However, I have realized we often downplay how powerful that is. Human possibility is not a limitation; it is a powerful tool in the hands of the willing soul. Human possibility is a God-given gift and ought to be honored and stewarded properly.

Like I stated before, perspective is everything. Our lack of control is a good thing. I mean really, God being in control is much more reliable than me going crazy trying to make sure all the pieces of my life fall in line. He gives each and every person a role to play, our basket of tools, and expects us to rise to the occasion and take responsibility for the life He has entrusted us with. Don't downplay human possibility; it's a gift from heaven.

I battled weight issues and food addiction for about fourteen years before I realized I am powerful beyond measure. What are you battling you don't feel capable of facing? What have you convinced yourself you are too weak to conquer or excel in? If there is any consolation in my story, allow it to be God is in control and He will empower you to do all that is humanly possible.

There is great comfort in knowing God only expects you to do that which He has given us the authority and jurisdiction to do. Leave everything else up to Him. Today is your day to conquer. Stop putting off your life. Leave the Monday mentality in the past and trust that God will equip you to do all that is necessary to win. But first, you have to relinquish control.

Actually, it's only relinquishing the belief you are in control.

CHAPTER 8

WEAPONS FOR THE FIGHT

When the biblical character David killed Goliath, he did so with a rock and slingshot. Just like David, we all have weapons we use to fight the daily battles of life. Once we have decided we will enter the fight, we must also be equipped to win.

Back in 2007 when I began my weight-loss journey, I didn't have a road map. I didn't have examples to show me the ropes on how to overcome obesity. However, as a result of the journey I have taken, I gained some weapons along the way.

As I went, I became aware of what it took for me to be able to continue strong. Though I did not have a road map with insight on helpful weapons, I became determined I would do my best to offer to others what I gained along the way. I want to give to others what I did not have.

Weapons for the Battle

Though my journey has been about weight loss, my goal is that as you read the book you realize the principles apply to any journey in life. Regardless of what your thing is the majority of the weapons necessary to fight the battles of life are consistent. Battles may come in various forms: goals to be accomplished, dreams to be fulfilled, addictions to overcome, assignments to complete. What I've realized is that in some way or another, there is always a battle to be fought and we must be equipped to do well in the fight.

My battle was overcoming obesity. I want to share insights on what I faced and how I learned to grow and overcome in the midst of it. Some of the weapons are general and applicable to various areas and some of my weapons are specific to the journey of obesity but can be modified for your specific battle. Here are ten weapons I've gained over the course of my four-year journey:

10 WEAPONS FOR THE FIGHT

1. A Made-Up Mind
2. Accountability
3. A Food Plan

4. A Workout Plan

5. Readiness

6. Inspiration

7. Goals

8. A Winner's Perspective

9. Consistency

10. A Break

A Made-Up Mind

Businessman Norman R. Augustine said, "Motivation will almost always beat mere talent."

In my world, motivation is called your why. I know I speak of this often throughout the book, but it's because having it is crucial to every single season of life. The why factor is essentially your guiding force. Success requires you to be tuned in and connected to the force. Being successful does not require a supernatural or extraordinary ability. It requires willingness.

You must be willing to cling to your motivation and refuse to let go. I've come to know the mind to be the strongest weapon I have in the fight of life. I'm a firm believer your actions are directly connected to how strong your mindset is.

For years I've lived defeated because I had convinced myself I was weak and powerless. I accepted a mentality of defeat. When I tapped into my why and chose to live in accordance to my hope and not constrained by my fears, I was able to thrive.

When your mind is altered, your decisions follow suit.

Everything you do or don't do in this life is connected to your mindset. Before I began my journey, I made up my mind that freedom was my only option. I didn't know where I was going, but one thing I was certain of, I had to leave where I was. A made-up mind says I'll do whatever it takes by any means necessary. A made-up mind says no matter how difficult the journey ahead, it's worth me enduring. A made-up mind focuses on the desired outcome and decides that though difficult or uncertain, the journey ahead will not hinder you from reaching your intended destination.

Having a why is the key element of a made-up mind. Your why narrows you in and gives you a focus. It helps to silence the noise around you and the noise that will attempt to invade your mind. Your why screams louder than your fears and concerns, and it grounds you, anchors you and strengthens you to move forward.

I suggest you know your why and always have it accessible.

Write it down, record it on a video, share it with friends, as long as you know what it is and you always have a means of reminding yourself. Keep close to your why, keep your mind guarded, focus, and you are bound to be very successful on this journey. I believe a made-up mind is the most important weapon in the fight. Everything else is a reflection of how connected you are to your why.

Accountability

One morning I was watching a DVD of my pastor preaching, and during his sermon he posed the questions, Who walks with you? Who shares this journey with you? Who speaks truth into your life? Who shares your struggles? To whom are you accountable?

These questions apply to so many areas of our lives. Accountability comes in various forms, but at the end of the day, we all need a system of support that aids in our success on the journey. What works for one person may not always work for another. However, the options are limitless, and there is something out there for each person. You just have to be willing to seek it out and ultimately apply the method that fits best for your personality and lifestyle.

Only pride will tell you you can do it alone, that you

don't need anyone. Pride and shame often keep us living our lives sheltered and guarded. But the most successful people, regardless of the arena of success, will tell you that accountability played a massive role in their achievement. Man, oh man, I thrive off accountability. It is so darn important to me. The human ego will keep you from having a support system, but the human ego will also set you and me up for failure, and none of us have time for failure.

I have a disclaimer to make. Accountability only works if you choose to work it. It is only successful if you actually avail yourself to it. No one or nothing can force you to be truthful, honest, and committed to your own goals and aspirations. A source of accountability is there to assist you in the process and to help you stay on track, but each person has to be committed. My systems of accountability have really helped to keep me on track, and I suggest everyone create a system that's best for them.

The most popular form of accountability is a person. I have all kinds of accountability partners. For the record, I am not saying just anyone can be your person. You have to choose people with whom you feel safe. Emotional safety is a must in my journey. I am way too fragile to just let anyone super close to me, but I've found a few safe people, and they have been really good for me.

My friend Chiyah used to work out with me all the time.

My old youth pastor Daven would literally meet me at the gym early in the morning to push me in my workouts. My sister and I would walk, ride bikes, and shop for healthy groceries together. We would even go to events, and I would ask her to make sure I didn't eat certain foods while I was there. If we went out with family or friends to a restaurant, we would split a meal to ensure I didn't overeat. These and so many more have walked alongside me in various seasons of my weight-loss journey to help me.

We all need help in staying the course. It doesn't make you weak to reach out for help. It makes you wise. A wise person acknowledges weaknesses and creates the environment necessary to ensure their personal success. It's just dumb to think you can become great all by yourself. Having people in your corner who will push you when you lack the desire to stick to your commitments is a great accountability source.

Like I stated before, there are different strokes for different folks. There are weight-loss groups and programs like Weight Watchers, one-on-one friends to check in with regularly, support groups like Eaters Anonymous, or online communities such as Lose It or My Fitness Pal. Some people use their personal trainer as their accountability or various means of social media. On my journey, YouTube and social media became a dominant source of accountability for me.

I knew that every Tuesday I was going to check in and that thought would motivate me throughout my week. I began that blog back in 2010, and from that point on, my social media following has really grown. Honestly, it's my greatest form of accountability because I just can't lie to thousands of people. It keeps me on my toes. When I feel myself falling off, I set a new goal and post it on my social media outlets, and my followers keep me accountable. As a result, this has become an amazing support system for me. To this very day, when I want to give up or give in, I think of my followers, and I decide to keep going. I realize I'm not only doing this for myself, but that as I live my life, I become an inspiration to others. They can look at my life and realize they too can overcome the seemingly impossible.

I gave two main examples of accountability in my life, but there are countless ways of incorporating this principle into your personal journey. Remember, you have to make the choice to be truthful, transparent, and committed to whichever avenue to which you choose to be connected. It works if you choose to work it. Do what is fitting for you, but just do something.

A Food Plan

I have often heard it said, "If you fail to plan, you plan to fail." Planning is essential. The odds of succeeding on this journey are greatly increased when you have a plan. I honestly believe weight loss is primarily eating and secondarily exercise. I call it the 70/30 rule. Seventy percent of weight loss comes from adjusting your diet, and thirty percent comes from incorporating physical activity into your life. I automatically began seeing weight drop off me when I became intentional about the way I ate. However, we live in a very fast-paced, non-stop, commuter-friendly society that isn't considerate of those attempting to live a healthy lifestyle.

Where I live, there are fast food restaurants on every corner, and convenient stores are extremely accessible. Therefore, planning out how you will eat and having the food accessible to you is a huge weapon on this fight. It takes some time to commit to the planning process, but once you've done the work, it makes your week much easier to conquer. My suggestions for planning in regards to eating are:

1. Write out your desired meals and snacks for the week.
2. Create a grocery list based on the meals and snacks.
3. Designate a day to shop and prepare for the week.
4. Once you arrive at the store, actually shop your list.
5. Prepare and pre-package your food for the week or at least for the next few days.

6. Keep healthy snacks in your car and at work.

7. When eating out, plan ahead. Review the menu. Go to the restaurant knowing what you will order. If possible, plan to split a meal or ask for half your food to be boxed to go at the beginning of your meal.

8. When eating in settings that you do not have control over what food is prepared or offered, focus on making the better choice and on portion control. You can't always control your environment, but you can control your choices within the environment.

You will get the hang of what works for you. Maybe you don't apply every single one of the suggestions at the start of your journey. You can incorporate change as you go. Nevertheless, the key is to plan ahead. The more you plan, the greater your outcomes will be. You minimize the opportunities to be caught off guard. However, just like accountability, it only works if you actually apply the plan to your life. Once you develop a plan, you must choose to stick to it in order to see the results yielded. Also, it's okay to modify your plan along the way. Examine what's working for your lifestyle and adjust appropriately as you go.

A Workout Plan

Just like having a food plan, I have a workout plan. I believe in life, we'll always have time for the things we deem important. The truth is, we don't create time or change it. Everyone has twenty-four hours in a day. The key to time is choosing for yourself what your priorities are and how they occupy your time.

We don't create time, we simply steward it. That being said, almost everything that is a priority in my life goes on my calendar. I schedule it because it's essential and I want to make sure I make room in my day for it to occur.

If someone were to open my calendar on my phone, they would see many of my priorities in life. I schedule everything from reading my Bible to catching up on lunch with a friend, to a reminder to call my grandma to check in on her or to drop by my mom's house just to let her know I'm still alive. I scheduled time to work on my book and the times I simply need to rest and have me time. I'm not saying I can't be spontaneous.

I am often very spontaneous, but I am also very intentional about making sure certain things happen in my life. For example, I tell people, we can talk about getting together and catching up on life as much as we want to, but if we don't lock down a time and put it in my calendar, it probably isn't happening.

Likewise, this is how I approach working out.

I schedule my workouts. Typically, I am an early-bird person when it comes to working out. I prefer to knock it out in the morning and go on with the rest of my day. I don't like going throughout the day thinking about the fact that I still have to work out. So like most other areas of life that are important to me, my planned workouts have their own slot on my schedule. When people say to me, I don't have time to work out, I simply reply, "You have time to do what you make time to do."

When your why is in place, when you've made up in your mind that your desired outcomes are worth fighting for, you re-adjust your life schedule to engage those activities that will aid you in the process of getting the results.

Readiness

My youth pastor often said, "If you stay ready, you don't have to get ready." Life throws unexpected curve balls our way, but if we're intentional in trying to stay two steps ahead, we are much more likely to succeed. I call this readiness. I learned early on I have to make health and fitness very accessible to me. I have to be alert, prepared, and ready to face the everyday battle for my life. I make small decisions that create a great impact on my day-to-day life. I try to make sure I'm ready for the battle.

Here are a few ways I make sure I'm ready:

- I keep snacks in my car. I never want to be out and about, get hungry and not have a healthy snack as an option. Once I get really hungry, I'm bound to grab any snack available to me to get rid of my hunger. Well, unfortunately my environment usually isn't conducive to my lifestyle. There are fast food restaurants, vending machines, convenience stores, and such that I'm often surrounded by, and they rarely have options that are suitable for my diet. Thus, as best as I can, I try to keep my own snacks handy.

- In addition to snacks, I try to keep workout clothes in the trunk of my car. I never know if a moment in the day may avail itself for me to get a workout in. I typically plan my workouts and stick to them, but there are times when the day doesn't turn out the way I'd scheduled it.

- I'm a member of a twenty-four-hour fitness center, and there are many locations. Therefore, I may find myself in an area of town, for any particular reason, and spot a gym, and I take advantage of the opportunity before me. I schedule my life, but I also plan for glitches in the schedule or for the day to not turn out in a way that I anticipated.

- The more equipped you are to face the day, the higher

the probability of being successful at the goals you set for yourself. Your readiness may not look like mine, but be sure you're ready to face the battle in a way that best suits your particular lifestyle. Those who are ready to face the battle are much more likely to win the war.

Inspiration

We all need a little inspiration from time to time. Inspiration is like an injection that gives you the boost to keep going. It comes in the form of songs, quotes, billboards, and even through people. It's the weapons of the fight that are geared toward building up your mind.

Your mind is a powerful tool in life. It can be your greatest asset or your worst enemy. It all comes down to what you do with it, how you treat it. I learned earlier on in the fight that my success or failure ultimately comes down to what I did or did not do with my mind, my thoughts.

It's not enough to simply tell a person to get rid of negative thoughts. That's not how the human mind works. The mind will always be filled with something. It will never remain a mass of empty space. You can't simply tell a person to stop a certain behavior or thought process. Instead, you must learn to fuel your mind with a lot of goodness, which will work to push out the negative thoughts. The reality is they simply can't occupy the same space, but the space will be occupied.

One of my favorite Bible verses states, "Finally brethren, whatever things are true, whatever things are noble, whatever things are just, whatever things are pure, whatever things are lovely, whatever things are of good report, if there is any virtue and if there is anything praiseworthy—meditate [think] on these things" (Philippians 4:8, New King James Version). Point blank, think on, meditate on, and keep in your mind the things that will equip you to actually overcome in this battle.

Have handy resources to empower you when you feel overwhelmed, defeated, hopeless, full of doubt, or just plain tired. Your why, which is your internal motivation, coupled with your external sources of inspiration offers you the second wind you need to keep going. For example, one of my whys is that I want to be able to shop for the clothes I want to wear. One of my external inspirations is a song entitled "Fighter" by Christiana Aguilera. I get out the bed in the morning and head to work out because I'm driven by my internal why. However, once I get to the gym, the song "Fighter" helps me to believe I'm strong and capable of conquering the battle ahead of me. It fuels my mind with goodness, with a belief I can do this. The inspiration couples with the motivation, and it manifests itself in my decision to keep going. We must conquer the battle in our mind.

I believe your mindset is one of the most important tools you have on the journey. Weight loss is like seventy percent nutrition and thirty percent exercise, but it's also one hundred mentality. No, that is not a perfect math equation, but it makes perfect sense to me. You'll make the necessary decisions in relation to food and activity when your mind is properly geared. I believe many people end up quitting on the journey, not because they don't know how to eat or exercise, but because they didn't put the work into building their minds.

Like any muscle, your mind has to be trained consistently, so what tools do you need to build your mind? Here are a few items I learned were necessary on my journey to overcoming obesity: empowering books, songs, scriptures, quotes, videos, movies, sermons, speeches, and people.

I suggest building your own resource bank of inspiration. As you go along your journey, note which elements have impacted you and write them down. I'm a person of routine. When I find something that works for me in a given area of life, I repeat it over and over. Begin building your list today.

Goals

Sometimes you have to switch things up in order to keep life exciting. You can do a thing long enough that it loses its excitement and it becomes mundane and boring. I had to lose more than one hundred pounds, and not only did I have to lose the weight, I had to maintain it. Along the journey, I learned in order to keep the journey alive and exciting, I had to set goals and challenges for myself. Though I'm a person of routine, the routine can get boring, and before I knew it, I'd fallen off altogether.

As a result of this happening, I started making goals and setting challenges. For example, I trained for a half marathon. Instead of just getting up every morning and jogging, I created an end goal—a challenge I could work toward. It made the process not seem never-ending and eternal. It gave me something to set my mind to and to work toward. My overall goal was health and fitness, but challenges along the way made the overall goal feel more tangible, and it helped me to feel more accomplished and successful.

I didn't start off with goals like the half marathon. I remember when I couldn't do a push-up, and I focused all my energy on getting up to doing ten. Now, I set goals such as five thousand push-ups in one month or challenging myself to drink one gallon of water every day for an entire month. Perhaps you don't work out at all, then you can set a goal to work out three times a week for an entire month. Instead of just saying, "I'm going to get healthier," you give yourself an actual goal to work toward that serves in the overall purpose of health and fitness.

Goals and challenges help you to keep from getting bored with doing the same thing, and they push you to challenge yourself and to stretch yourself. The more you challenge yourself, the more you see yourself conquering those things that once seemed impossible. You begin to feel stronger and to see yourself in a new light. You grow in your confidence.

One thing I've realized on this journey is that when you see yourself conquering in one difficult area of life, like weight loss, it encourages you to start tackling the other areas of life that also seem hard or impossible. For example, writing this book is huge for me. However, I think, *If I can lose 180 pounds naturally, surely I can write this book.* It doesn't mean the book writing process isn't a challenge. It simply means the idea of a challenge doesn't paralyze me. I now know I can do difficult things and they won't take me out. I encourage you to set goals and challenges for yourself. Keep life exciting and give yourself the opportunity to conquer in the face of difficulty over and over and over.

A Winner's Perspective

Whenever I offer advice on how to be successful in the weight-loss journey, I'm pretty frank: "You have to set yourself up to win." Sometimes the strongest thing you can do is to know your own weaknesses and guard yourself against them. The reality is we're going against a current. I learned early on that it wasn't just about my ability to resist. I had to learn how to not even put myself into some tempting circumstances because the odds were, I would probably succumb to the temptation. A winner's perspective says, "I'll do whatever it takes for me to be successful to win the fight."

One of my favorite restaurants is The Cheesecake Factory, particularly for their bread. In the early stages of my weight-loss journey I realized it was almost impossible for me to resist eating an entire basket of bread. I learned I wasn't strong enough to simply use portion control. I'm stronger now. However, it was too new for me and I hadn't built up the ability to resist early in my journey. I would tell the waitress to remove the bread basket. I didn't want to fall into temptation, so I decided the best option was not to have the bread around. I was willing to go the distance to have a "by any means necessary" attitude.

I really enjoy Cheez-Its. They're one of my all-time favorite snacks. I've realized I can't have a box of Cheez-Its in my home. Before you know it, what began as just a little bit turns into the entire box being gone in one day. It's not that I can't ever have them. I can have a snack size bag here and there, but in order to ensure I don't devour an entire box, the best plan is for me to just not have the box in my home.

If I want to win in this battle, I must know what my weaknesses are and limit the opportunity to fall prey to the temptation. It's like the alcoholic who goes into a bar and says, "I just won't drink." No, my friend, that's dumb. The best decision is to not go to the bar, to limit the environments that are ultimately detrimental to your progress. Sometimes this means changing the people you spend the bulk of your time with. You may have to get new friends or decide to journey alone for a particular season of life. You do whatever is necessary to create an environment that supports your desire to win the battle. It takes a winner's perspective.

Consistency

I have this belief that consistency beats intensity. If you practice anything for a long enough time, you become good at it. It doesn't mean it becomes easy. It means you have learned how to do it, even when it's difficult, and how to become successful at doing a hard thing.

My mentor calls me a weight-loss expert. I never used to consider myself an expert because I know the daily struggle. However, I realized that being an expert doesn't mean it is not a challenge. On the contrary, I've learned how to face the challenge and allow it to produce in me what it's supposed to produce. This happens through consistency.

You don't become good at a thing overnight. You work at it. You decide not to give up—to keep going and to allow it to become part of your routine of life. Weight loss, health, and nutrition are not a destination. Even once you've lost the weight you want, in order to maintain the weight loss, you learn to create a new lifestyle for yourself. Consistency is built over time.

It took me four years, but I was able to develop a new way of living for myself. Many people try these quick and intense programs, but they're not a lasting, realistic, lifestyle transition. I didn't become a workout fanatic in one month. I began with one thing, and I was consistent at it. Over time, I added more to my plate. I began working out, eating differently, and incorporating new challenges in my life.

I truly believe consistency is more beneficial in the long run than trying to conquer the world all in one day. Pick one or two areas and build a routine from that, and over time add to your program. Change doesn't happen overnight. You can't have a lifestyle for twenty years then think that because you've been working out for one week, everything is supposed to change. Give yourself grace and choose to be consistent. Over time, the results will yield in your favor.

A Break

Sometimes you just need a "whoosah!" You can't always be on the grind. In life it's healthy to just step back, ease up, and take a break. When it comes to weight loss, I realized this is a lifestyle and it's only maintainable if you incorporate realistic expectations. Allow yourself the space to enjoy and engage the treats, which may come in different forms on your journey, but allow them to take their proper place.

For example, if you're writing a book, though you need

to be consistent in the process, you may need to take one day a week where you aren't writing and you simply go to the beach or the movies or spend time with friends. That break also serves to fuel you with the extra strength you need to get back to the grind. I learned this when it came to my weight loss. Some people have cheat days or cheat meals. Personally, I love frozen yogurt with toppings. They say, "Disneyland is the happiest place on earth." I say *yogurtland* is the happiest place on earth. I probably eat it about once a week on average. It's just my thing. I also like fries, and that isn't going to change. I'm not going to lie to myself and say I'm never going to eat fries again. I have them every so often. To tell myself I'll never enjoy fries or frozen yogurt again is a lie.

When I lie to myself, I then set myself up for failure because I've placed unrealistic expectations out there. That's the main reason I'm not a fan of extreme diets that have you cut out all the "bad" stuff from your life. It doesn't teach you how to maintain a lifestyle that allows you to enjoy the foods that are pleasurable to you. You lose the weight and then what? You never learned how to eat the foods you enjoy in a moderate form. You now live in an all-or-nothing type of mentality, and you end up putting the weight back on.

Trust me, I've seen it happen to so many people around

me. I am a fan of temporary diets for the sake of cleansing or things of that sort, but you have to know you won't live this way forever, and you must create a lifestyle you can maintain. I've learned the most successful lifestyle is one that allows me to occasionally have my treats. To be successful on this journey, I have to give myself a break. Take a break from the routine, then hop right back on. Actually, I like to consider the break being part of the routine. Create a routine that incorporates the whoosah. Your breaks in life may not look like mine, but everyone needs one.

Know Your Weapons

These are ten weapons that stood out to me along my journey. Try them out and see if they work for you as well. Even if your journey isn't specifically about weight loss, the overarching principles can still be applied to your situation. You can incorporate my weapons, but I also suggest you pay attention to your own. As you go on your journey, you'll discover those elements of life that help you to fight the good fight and to do it well. Write those weapons down and repeat them over and over. Share your insights with others and become a support system on their journey to overcoming in the face of what seems impossible. The more weapons we have, the more equipped we are to winning the battle. You grow in your strength to overcome the Monday mentality.

CHAPTER 9

OWN THIS MOMENT

You may be familiar with the biblical character Moses. In the book of Exodus, God came to Moses with an assignment. At that time, Moses' people were slaves in Egypt, and God had purposed that Moses would be the one who would confront pharaoh and usher his people out of slavery and into a Promise Land that God had designated for them to enter.

When God visited Moses and gave him the task to go and speak to pharaoh about the deliverance of the people, Moses immediately responded in fear. He began to share with God why he was inadequate for the assignment at hand. Moses had a speech impediment, and he had determined his own weakness counted him out. We are often like Moses. Some-times we decide the very thing we were destined to achieve, we don't have what it takes to carry out the task. We suggest to God the resources we currently have are simply not enough.

When I was 356 pounds, I believed I couldn't lose the weight, especially since I didn't have an example before me. I thought it was impossible. Like Moses, I was convinced I was inadequate, that the task before me was just way too much to handle. I'm sure you too can relate to this feeling. I think it's a universal experience. At some point in life, we all have to face the thing that seems like it's too much for us to handle, and our desire will be to not move forward. We will fight in this war between moving forward with courage versus remaining stuck and paralyzed by fear.

Even as you read through this book, you probably started thinking of your list of what you need to conquer, and the thought of the tasks most likely produced some feelings of anxiety. At least that's how it often happens in my life, and it seemed to be the case with Moses as well. It's a great task and accomplishment to be done, we just don't feel like we're the ones for the job. The idea sounds great until it dawns on us that it's the idea we are supposed to live out.

It's like taking a shower. How many times have we hopped in the shower and during that time we thought of all kinds of wonderful ideas, visions, dreams and aspirations? The shower seems to be that time for me. I begin dreaming and thinking of the things I could do with my life and the amazing accomplishments that can be made. However, something happens between the shower and the time I'm ready to walk out the house. In the shower I feel unstoppable, but between the shower and my front door, fear, doubt and all of my limitations come to mind and like Moses, I begin to battle that overwhelming beast called inadequacy. We feel like we are just not enough.

Be encouraged!

What we often want is for the weakness to leave us, but what Moses had to realize was his weakness did not make him inadequate. No, God was with him, and if God was the one to call him to accomplish the task, then surely God was the one responsible for ensuring Moses had all he needed to be successful.

Moses' speech impediment was not a surprise to God. My obesity was not a surprise to God. God knew my daddy was going to die well before I did, and whatever you are currently facing, God already knows that as well. We all are, in some way, just like Moses.

As the story continued, Moses rose to the occasion and accomplished the task God had set before him, to deliver the people out of slavery. And in this very moment, you too—limitations and all—can be successful. Your resources don't need to shift, your perspective does. My circumstances didn't have to change; I changed my thoughts about what I already had right before me. When I had to lose the weight, I didn't immediately gain a trainer, a dietician and a guide to weight loss. I started walking more and driving less. My perspective changed on what was already at my fingertips. The same God who calls you to accomplish the task, will equip you with the strategy to do so. However, it requires a shift in your attitude toward the circumstance and your own abilities.

As Moses set his focus above on the call of God, the obstacles before him began to not have as much value as they did before. The obstacles did not go away, they simply no longer had the power that Moses had once given them. Moses gave his weaknesses the opportunity to hinder and paralyze him from action. But Moses also decided to trust God, and that trust built over time, and he was able to experience all kinds of miracles in his life. God took the ordinary resources of life and turned them into miracles as He journeyed with Moses and the people.

As long as God had Moses' heart, Moses had God's provision. When you shift your thinking from deciding inadequacy counts for everything and instead trust that even with your inadequacies, you can be successful, your momentum will grow and you will begin to conquer. Remember, this is a day-by-day, moment-by-moment, decision-by-decision journey.

Another Challenge from God

Many of us can relate to Moses or perhaps you feel more like Joshua. We discussed Joshua early in the book and his confrontation with fear versus courage. On their way to the land that God promised to give them, Moses died. Though they were out of slavery, they had not yet reached their new home and all of a sudden, their leader dies. I often find my own story in the middle of this tragic scene. I have found hope in this passage because it is often how our lives occur. The people were faced with what seemed to be an impossible task. Their leader died.

Joshua was like a son to Moses. You can say perhaps Moses was Joshua's mentor. Well, all of a sudden, the mentor died and God visited Joshua. In Joshua chapter 1, the text tells us that God came to Joshua and announces to him that Moses died, and now it is Joshua's time to lead the people the remainder of the way. If I were Joshua, I would have immediately felt afraid and out of my league. I'm sure Joshua was under the impression

Moses was going to be the one to lead them all the way to the intended destiny so when God comes to Joshua with the news of Moses' death, it was a shock to him. I would have even suggested to God, it might be time to resurrect Moses because he has to lead us the rest of the way. Not only was his mentor, the leader, dead but also now God is expecting Joshua to assume responsibility. Knowing the human mind so well, God immediately reassured Joshua. He reminded Joshua how just like when Moses felt weak and not equipped to do his job, God was going to be strength for Joshua in his current predicament.

God pulled from his history with Moses to serve as an example to Joshua that He would not abandon him in the middle of great difficulty. Just as He was with Moses, He will also be with Joshua. God then commanded Joshua to be strong and courageous. Remember, courage does not mean you don't have fear. Of course Joshua had a reason to be afraid, so it was fair for fear to be on the scene. However, God reminded Joshua of what to do with the fear. He told him to be courageous, to move forward in the face of it. Why did God tell Joshua to have courage? Simple, because God was with Joshua just like he was with Moses.

Allow me to be your Moses. You may be wondering if you can really move forward with the desires that are pressing on your heart. For so long, you may have allowed fear to win the battle. You may be stuck in the place of calculating all of your inadequacies and wondering if you really are capable of moving forward. Can I be your Moses? I believe in you. I know what it is like to be where you are. I know what it means to have a list of desired conquests, to dream in the shower and then to fight anxiety on my way out of the front door. I know you. I tell myself every reason why I am not good enough. And God has to remind me over and over that my list of deficiencies does not disqualify me from being successful. The only reason why I have gained any level of success that I have in my life is solely attributed to the fact that I shifted my focus off me and I placed my gaze on the God who has called me and designed my life to be fruitful and abundant.

Will you allow me to be your Moses? As you seek to abandon the Monday mentality and move forward with the destiny of your life, perhaps you too, like Joshua, need a point of reference. You read my story and now it's time for you to continue forward in your story, to allow the next chapter to be one of which you are proud, not because it's perfect but because you pushed forward in purpose with courage. It's time for you to live your life and to own your moment. It's time for you to write down your why and allow it to fuel you to take the next step. As Joshua gained strength from God's journey with Moses, it is my hope and prayer this book has allowed you to gain strength from my journey with God as God says to you, *"For I will be with you as I was with Liana. I will not fail or abandon you. Only, be strong and courageous!"*

CHAPTER 10

FREQUENTLY ASKED QUESTIONS

After I lost one hundred pounds I faced great discouragement because I was tired and overwhelmed, and I wanted the journey to be over. It was exciting that I lost so much weight, but I grew weary because I still had more distance to cover.

Through blogging and the various social media outlets, my online community has grown into a dynamic support system and basis for encouragement. A few years ago, when I began writing this book, I asked my online community if there were any specific questions they wanted me to answer. This chapter is dedicated to many of those questions. I wouldn't be where I am today if it weren't for the amazing followers I have, so I consider it a privilege and an honor to answer these questions. I hope I encourage more people to commit to the journey and to take ownership of their lives. Read and be encouraged!

What size were you before and what size are you now?

At the beginning of my journey, I was wearing a women's size twenty-eight, and today I wear a women's eight/ten. When I consider how far I've come, it still amazes me.

What kick-started your journey?

My pastor once posed the question, "Have you ever been so far down that you jumped up and touched the bottom of down?" Well, that's pretty much how I felt. I was at my low, I felt trapped, and I was finally ready to be free. I was dying on the inside. I felt like I wasn't living but merely existing. I wanted more out of life.

For years my obesity controlled me. It was the primary factor in every single decision I made, and it was wearing me to pieces. I eventually decided I was worth more and that I was willing to give myself a chance at living. I was pushing four hundred pounds, and it scared me to action. I didn't know where I was going or how I was going to get there. One thing is for sure, I knew I needed to leave where I was, so my journey began.

What was your daily routine when you began and how has it changed?

Before I began my weight-loss journey, I lacked discipline. I ate whatever I wanted whenever I wanted. I rarely ever exercised. When I first began changing, I decided to take it step by step. I didn't change everything all at one time. It was a gradual change. Initially, I took sodas and juice out of my diet and committed to drinking water only.

Today, though it still requires intentionality, I'm more disciplined. Being healthy is a lifestyle. I work out about five to six times a week, and primarily water is my only liquid. I drink coffee as well, but overall, I've completely changed my relationship to food. I don't eat a lot of fried or fatty foods, fast food restaurants, and desserts. I have my cheat items from time to time, and I cook a lot for myself. I eat mostly protein, vegetables, fruits, whole grains, and legumes. I'm intentional about when I eat out and the locations I choose. I've learned this journey is a lifestyle. It isn't a quick fix or a momentary diet. It's a decision to completely commit to a new way of thinking and thus, living.

Did it hurt to move or walk when you were your heaviest?

Life was definitely much more uncomfortable when I was obese.

I was not constantly in pain. However, activities such as climbing stairs and running required me to exert a lot of energy, and I often felt winded from doing minor tasks. It didn't hurt for me to walk, but if I ran, my legs would immediately begin to hurt, especially in my shins. As I lost the weight, it became much more comfortable for me to engage in everyday activities.

How did you change your diet when you hit a plateau?

Initially, I didn't count my calories. I was aware of them and took them into consideration as I was making choices, but I never put myself on a caloric regimen. One way I continued to lose weight when I experienced a plateau was I used a website called Lose It, and it helped me know how many calories I should be eating a day in order to lose the weight I wanted to lose.

Also, I would switch up my workout routine. I wouldn't do the same thing every day. Switching up helped my body to not get accustomed to one workout. Our bodies have a great memory, and over time, the same results will not be produced from doing the same routine over and over. Change in routine, both eating and exercise, helps your body to continue to change and drop the pounds.

As you got farther along, did it become easier or more difficult?

Both. It becomes easier and more difficult in different ways. It becomes easier because as you remain consistent over time, you begin to develop a new lifestyle—a new pattern for yourself. Everything new is difficult, and it takes time to adjust to. Your life begins to alter and your decisions become more natural. You still have to remain intentional, but it becomes easier because over time you learn what works best for you, and you incorporate those things into your life so you're able to set yourself up to win.

For example, I know the best time to work out for me is in the morning. That way, I don't have to go throughout my entire day thinking, *Man, I still have to work out.* I'm able to feel successful, which sets the tone for my entire day and impacts the decisions and perspective I have on how I approach my day. Mornings work for me, and now that I know that, it's easier for me to plan out my day in a manner that ensures my personal success.

On the flip side, it gets difficult because weight loss and maintenances are two different things. Once you lose the weight, it's hard to keep it off. Many people lose weight, but the battle becomes realizing the habits that got them to lose the weight need to be the same habits to keep the weight off. We are often okay with doing something for a given amount of time, but realizing the commitment is a lifetime one is the true test of success. It indeed is difficult, but I've learned it's worth it. I've learned it through experience—through seasons of gaining weight because I slacked on my habits and I did not like the way it caused me to feel. The battle is the daily one of choosing to fight for myself over and over and over, one decision at a time.

Where are your favorite grocery stores to shop now?

Trader Joe's, Sprouts Farmer's Market, and Target are my staples for grocery shopping.

Where are your favorite clothing stores to shop?

I love Nike, H&M, and Target.

How do you handle the fear of going back to your old size?

This thought visits me frequently. The truth of the matter is I still love food, and sometimes I get overwhelmed with the thought, *What if I can't do this forever?* I realize I got where I am by making one decision at a time. I don't need to focus on the next ten years from now or whether I can maintain this lifestyle forever. God didn't give me forever. He gave me this moment. My job is to live in the moment and to steward it well.

I tell myself, "Liana, victory over obesity is in the decisions you make moment by moment." God gives me enough to conquer today. Tomorrow will take care of itself. I lost 180 pounds by making moment-by-moment decisions, and that's how I'm going to continue to conquer.

Sometimes there were good decisions and sometimes not-so-good ones, but the best decision I've always made was to move forward past fear, disappointment, doubt, discouragement, and hopelessness. I press forward in my right now, and it helps to take away the fear of facing an unknown tomorrow.

Is it fun to exercise now? If so, when did it become fun?

For the most part, the only exercises I consider to be fun are dancing, swimming, and jumping double Dutch. Overall, exercise isn't fun to me, but I enjoy both the physical and psychological benefits of exercise. Physically, I am getting stronger and sexier. The psychological benefits to exercise are really great as well. When I exercise, I feel strong, capable, powerful, athletic, resilient, and unstoppable. I am engaging in activities that once felt overwhelming and impossible to me. It may not always be fun, but it is always worth it.

Where did all the swag come from?

This is by far my favorite question. I was born with it! You can't create it; you simply exude it. Honestly, I believe swag is nothing more than confidence. I've learned to simply be me and to be confident that who I am is sufficient. I'm not walking around waiting for others to approve of who I am in order to believe I'm amazing just as I am. I'm comfortable with myself, and it allows me to be free to be. My swag is a reflection of my ability to say, "It isn't about validation from everyone around me. There is only one Liana, and I'm going to give her the opportunity to shine." I'm committed to being the best me, and it's an inexplicable feeling.

Have people's reactions changed toward you since the weight loss?

For the most part, people are very loving and supportive. I think everyone, including me, is pretty shocked at what I've done because most of us have never seen it done before. Overall, people treat me pretty well. I know I have those low-key haters—people who make comments here and there about not believing I lost weight the natural way, but I really don't give them much room in my mind. I have limited mental energy, and I choose to use it in a direction that's going to produce the maximum amount of fruit. I'm blessed to say the same friends I had when I was obese are the same friends I have now, including some new ones. This includes the best friend I spoke of earlier in the book.

Even though the nature of our friendship changed and we are not as close as we used to be, she still is and always will be considered family to me. Her family is my family and vice versa.

When people encounter drastic weight-loss change, I've heard them say their friends changed and began to treat them differently, but fortunately that's not my story. My circle has grown, but I don't think that's because I've lost weight. I think that's because I try my best to be a genuine, authentic, transparent, loving, fun person, and that's attractive to people.

As far as men are concerned, I get more attention—not a lot, but more than before. I don't think that's solely because of weight loss either. I have a new confidence, and I think when you love yourself and are confident in who you are, it draws people. Even after losing the weight, I didn't always have this confidence, and I still struggle with it now. It's a process—a journey. As I grow in my sense of self, I think it attracts people to me.

How do you remain motivated during your weight-loss journey when people around you did not adopt your new lifestyle?

Honestly, I had tunnel vision. I was so committed to being free that I was willing to do any and everything necessary to ensure that. Initially, I avoided many social eating contexts. I would cook for myself, eat at places I knew had choices for me such as El

Pollo Loco or Chipotle. I kept healthy choices on me or in close proximity so I didn't have to default to what others were eating. There were times when I was out with friends, I would literally get food from another location and then bring it to wherever my friends were eating. I was not bashful or ashamed of taking the necessary actions to set myself up to succeed.

Over time, people began to respect my journey, and they would initiate making accommodations to ensure there were things I could eat. If it were a family dinner or celebration, the host would make sure there were items available for me to eat. My family and community did not really change their eating habits, initially, but they loved and respected me enough to make sure I had opportunities to remain diligent in my endeavors.

How have you managed to fight through vacations and life interruptions?

I was real with myself. For example, I went on an all-you-can-eat cruise with my friends. I allowed vacations to be the exception to the rule and not the rule itself. I didn't relinquish all sense of control, but I loosened the reigns on myself. I enjoyed the small moment in time and then hopped back to my routine once I returned home. It's a lifestyle for me. It is unrealistic to think I'm going to eat salads and drink protein shakes every day of my life. Once I realized this entire new phase was a lifestyle, then I was able to accept that even vacations and cheat days are a part of it. I plan for my vacations and cheat days. If I know I'm going to loosen up a little, then the decisions leading up to and following those days are modified to offset the effects of them.

Did you set phase goals along the way?

I have absolutely set goals along the way. It helped me when the bigger picture seemed way too unattainable. For example, I initially focused on simply getting out of the three hundreds. As I made small goals, step by step, it allowed me to look back over the course of time and see how much I accomplished. As I noticed how successful I had been over time, it gave me the fuel to keep going. I believe in making small, attainable goals and choosing to conquer daily. It's a journey, so it was key for me to pace myself.

Who are the main people who kept you going—helped you to not give up?

I must say, I have been blessed with a great support system. Initially, I was not vocal or public with my weight loss. I simply started making changes and people began to notice the weight dropping off, and they would say encouraging, supportive comments when they saw me. These were typically people from my church or in my family. There are way too many people to name. My family has been nothing but supportive. They were verbally affirming and would make food accommodations for me to let me know they saw how much I was trying and they wanted to come along and support me. My auntie Mickey is the main person who did this. We have a lot of family parties and functions at her house, and she would literally make sure there was food for me to eat. She will never know how valuable that was for me. It made me feel seen.

My church has been my safe haven—the place I've always turned to when I needed to feel safe. The men and women there have showered me with love and support. However, there are a few people who were a little more hands-on in the process:

- My friend Chiyah has walked with me every step of the way. She was there when I was obese and encouraged me to lose weight when I mentioned being tired of being fat. She was there when *The Biggest Loser* denied me and I thought I couldn't go farther. She actually helped me come up with the name WatchQueenLose for my blog, and she allowed me to break down when I didn't make the show and didn't think I could continue. She was there to do my first workout with me when I decided to continue past the disappointment. She has been my rock on this journey.

- An amazing man named Daven Baptiste has been nothing but supportive. He walked up to me one day on my journey and said to me, "You are slacking off. I can tell you're slowing down. Don't quit." I don't know how he knew, but it was obvious, and he loved me enough to challenge me to stay the course. Not only did he challenge me, but also came alongside in a season of the journey and would work out with me to push me.

- A woman who is like a second mother to me, Angie, never, ever made me feel inadequate or less than for being obese, and the minute I told her I wanted to lose weight, she bought me some sneakers and began giving me food and workout suggestions. For a year I became a vegetarian because Angie suggested I try it out. I'm not still a vegetarian, but I learned that year that my body doesn't digest beef and pork well. She has been a great support for me practically and emotionally.

- My sister—my oh-so-irreplaceable sister—Jana, has been by my side. Moving in with her has been one of the best decisions I've ever made. We work out together, and we eat alike, so it helps us to keep each other accountable. She doesn't struggle with weight like me, but she's still a health-conscious person and that helps me. She makes it easier for me to do well. Also, I ask her to hold me accountable when I feel like I'm slipping, and she does just that. I feel safe with my sister, and not many people can say that.

- My mentor, Dr. Nicole LaBeach, encouraged my inner man a lot. It was like she saw something in me the day she met me, and she has consistently reminded me of my greatness and strength. She spoke life into me before I ever began the journey. She encouraged me to conquer fear by living in lieu of it, and it's like she always had an on-time word from God that fueled me when I felt weak. She's pretty amazing in my book.

- My dad has been my silent strength. He has caused me to realize how silence can be the loudest voice of love. There is not a day in my life that I remember my dad ever mentioning my weight, and that has spoken volumes to me. It has encouraged me on my journey because it caused me to believe I have nothing to prove to him or anyone else. Ultimately, he loves me, and that love doesn't waver with my size but is solid and unmovable. It has anchored me because it has caused me to believe this journey is about showing myself I'm the wonderful person he already knew me to be. I believe my dad modeled God's love for me—pure acceptance.

- Last but definitely not least is my mom who is my biggest fan. Oh my goodness, I can't believe how much she believes in me. If you leave it up to my mom, I am superwoman. She just looks at me and says, "Li Li, I can't believe you are my daughter." She says that all the time. She thinks I'm unstoppable, and it makes me believe I actually am. My mom is convinced of my power and strength, and it keeps me going. I motivate her to be healthy, and that motivates me to remain healthy. It seems awkward for your own mom to look up to you, but hey, I'm honored to pour back into the lives that have made me the woman I am. She says, "Li Li, you have found your resolve, and most people need to find theirs."

There are just way too many people to mention—from gym instructors, professors, classmates, peers, close friends, church members, Facebook followers, people in my community, mentees, mentors, and the list goes on. I've been blessed with an abundant community of love and support.

Did you ever want to give up? How did you encourage yourself to keep pushing?

Oh, I absolutely have faced moments of wanting to just throw in the towel. I have my why before me, and when I wanted to quit, I reminded myself of why I began the journey. Also, photos of how far I have come encourage me because they remind me of my strength. My YouTube videos are also great because they give me a walk down memory lane—a reminder of how in the past when I had no idea of how well I would do and then I see myself on the other side of the hurdle.

My doubt and hesitation about the future was always comforted by how God had brought me thus far, and it fueled me to continue. My own progress became a great source of encouragement for me, not to mention the songs, sermons, quotes, and friends who would always come along the journey at the exact moment in time when I needed it most. It was nothing but God's timing that kept me going when I felt too weak to continue.

How do I get back up? How do you overcome setbacks?

I talk to myself a lot. I'm very honest and real with myself. When I started my weight-loss journey I promised myself that no matter what, I would always be truthful with myself. That has been crucial for me. It keeps me from staying down when I fall. That being said, when I have setbacks, I eventually get to the point when I pause and have a talk with myself— "Liana, you want this. You've come way too far to quit. You never want to be fat again. You never want to feel the weight and the burden of the life you once had. You do care, and you can do this. You have to do this. The reality is you won't enjoy life if you choose to give up. You will constantly be unhappy and unsatisfied with compromise, complacency, and mediocrity. Get back up and keep going. It doesn't matter how bad you've messed up, you always have the next decision to make, and that next decision is truly the determining factor."

Anyone can go through a season of success and blessing and still feel empty because we forget God is the only one who fills the void, so the question becomes, "How can we stay in a place of complete dependence on Him, while everyone around us is praising us for our successes?"

My success is a reflection of the work God is doing in my life. So when people are acknowledging how well I've done, I translate that as, "God, Your work is really evident." God likes doing great things in our lives, and He loves it when others recognize it. It is my duty to honor the work He is doing. I am utterly aware of my weaknesses. I choose not to live a façade but to be honest with myself about my flaws and shortcomings. The more aware I am of my deficiencies, the more grateful I am of God's work in me and on my behalf. Thus, my life becomes a testimony of what God can do when you submit to His processes. I think that's why God allows us to have some struggles and He doesn't remove them all; it requires a level of dependency on Him that our successes are inevitably connected to. Thus, the moment we let go of our connection to God, we enter a downward spiral.

Do you notice a difference in your clarity of mind now that you have lost the weight?

Overcoming obesity has developed confidence. I have this newfound sense of possibility. What used to seem impossible no longer does. I have clarity in the sense that mental blocks and barriers are not as prevalent in my life because I've been able to witness myself conquer what was once inconceivable to me. Yes, I have more clarity because my mind is not clouded by doubt, fear, and defeat but rather I have focused on being exceptionally great because I have chartered territory few ever have, and I have made a believer out of myself. Now, that is crazy! The idea that I've done something exceptional and that I'm peculiar were not realities I thought I would ever actually exemplify. I've considered it in the past, but only as a passing thought. Now, I am fully convinced I don't have limitations, and that brings peace and clarity to my mind.

Are there any scriptures you kept reading or reciting throughout this journey?

I have a few rock scriptures that have carried me through this journey:

- "I can do all things through Christ who strengthens me" (Philippians 4:13).
- "Now the Lord is the Spirit, and where the Spirit of the Lord is, there is liberty" (2 Corinthians 3:17).
- "Who the Son sets free, is free indeed" (John 8:36).
- "The Spirit of the Lord God is upon me, because the Lord has anointed me to bring good news to the poor; he has sent me to bind up the brokenhearted, to proclaim liberty to the captives, and the opening of the prison to those who are bound" (Isaiah 61:1).
- "But he said to me, 'My grace is sufficient for you, for my power is made perfect in weakness.' Therefore I will boast all the more gladly of my weaknesses, so that the power of Christ may rest upon me" (2 Corinthians 1:9).

When you were in the midst of losing the weight, was there a point where you had to overcome something personally within yourself?

I had to overcome the idea I am not enough. I also had to overcome the idea I was working to become someone I thought I already wasn't. I realized I needed to see myself as great already and the process was in order to see it actualized in my life. Basically, I had to overcome the idea I needed to become someone other than the girl I already was. The problem wasn't she wasn't in me, rather it was I wasn't allowing her to flourish. My value, identity, and substance were created by God and stamped as good the moment I entered this world. My own distorted view of myself, as well as images reinforced in society caused me to think otherwise. Thus, this process helped me to overcome the idea I wasn't sufficient. My own brilliance is what I had to tap in to and not the desire to become someone different. I didn't become someone new. I blossomed.

Now that you've shed many layers and the person you've always known/felt was inside has surfaced, is she anything like you knew/visualized she'd be and look?

I didn't have an image of what size I would be. I had no idea where I was going or what the result would look like. I just knew I had to leave where I was, and it has been the greatest journey

I've ever ventured to take. As far as personality is concerned, I've simply unleashed the beast that has always been deep inside of me. There was this trapped lioness begging to be let out, and I gave her that chance. She would surface, but I would tame her because of fear and all of my insecurities, but now I let her roam, and if people don't like her, so what.

I would rather have five friends who love the authentic me than five hundred that celebrate a façade. I now take on life and its challenges. Sure, fear still surfaces, but the difference is I no longer allow it to paralyze me. I recognize it, and I face the fear, and it has made me so much stronger than I ever thought I would be. I finally love being me, and that's worth celebrating.

ACKNOWLEDGEMENTS

This section will never do justice to the community of women and men, via social media and in person who have been in my life, cheering me on, supporting me, loving me, and even correcting me (when necessary). *Monday Never Comes* is not my book alone, but our book!

Mom, thank you for being my model of what it looks like to fight for your life, for making your children the reason to never give up, and for remaining resilient in the face of adversity. I am certain that you were my first encounter with a true fighter.

My sister, Jana, thank you for your selflessness. You work towards my dreams as if they are your very own; I am grateful.

My family, you are truly my foundation. You have loved

me regardless of my size. I was always just "Li Li" to you. Because of your validation, I knew at a young age that I was something special in this world. Mine is a large family. Sims, Smith, Pigford, Ofumbi, Fields, Giles, Datcher and Williams families, you mean the world to me!

Dr. Nicole LaBeach, my mentor straight from the throne of God, your love is constant and persistent. I could write a whole book based solely upon how much I have learned from you. I am a better pastor and mentor because of your presence in my life. The commitment and love I have for the kids of the Takeover Youth Ministry and for every single one of my mentees, I first saw in you.

Dr. C, you are *the* greatest therapist. My world, the world, is a better place because God put you in it. You never condemned me for my mistakes; rather you created a sanctuary for me where I was free to fail without fear of judgment. You continue to demonstrate courage in the face of suffering. I am determined to share with others the gifts you have showered upon me.

Bishop Ulmer and my FCBC family, you rescued a broken, lonely girl and cultivated a confident, powerful woman. I love pastoring at FCBC simply because I have the privilege of pouring back into the place that has given me so much. More than a church, you are my home.

Bishop Sheridan McDaniel, Pastor Steven Johnson, Pastor Luscious Hicks, Varick Williams, Michael Anthony and Melvin Walker, you have been excellent fathers to me. In your own way, each of you has made me feel seen, protected, and cherished.

Alain Datcher, Joy Williams, Joi Madison, Victor Gabriel, Shalom Bako, Wengel Haile, Jasmine Jordan, Gail Dvorak, Pastor Monique Robinson, Pastor Shanthra Sparks, Kelli King-Jackson, Pastor Yolanda Williams, Sonya Byous, Makebra Bridges and Chiyah Lawrence I would not have had the strength to finish this book if it were not for you.

My Biola Family in general, and Michelle and Michael Anthony in particular, the time I spent on campus and with you has served to make me the leader, friend, and advocate that I am today.

Daven Baptiste, you took my vision and brought it to life. Thank you for believing in me and for contributing your phenomenal skills to *Monday Never Comes*. I love you!

Chandra Sparks Splond, I know there is a God because He sends people like you into my life just to remind me that He loves me and will always supply me with His best. Your final touches on this book have truly made the difference.

Daddy, when you died I wanted to give up. The thought that you can still see me living helps to keep me going. I hope I make you proud.

My God, my source, my strength, my anchor, my hope, my joy, my peace, my happiness, my friend, and most importantly, my Savior, there are no words simply gratitude for your unmerited and unconditional love!

THANK YOU! *Monday Never Comes* wouldn't exist if it weren't for you!